GATHERED AROUND THE
CAMPFIRE

S'MORES & STORIES UNDER THE STARS

MELODY A. CARLSON
ARTWORK BY MICHAL SPARKS

HARVEST HOUSE PUBLISHERS
EUGENE, OREGON

Contents

Dear fellow campers,

Although I grew up with a single mom who wasn't very campy or outdoorsy, I've always loved being out in nature. And despite somewhat limited childhood camp experiences with friends and relatives, I always nurtured a secret dream to become a real camper someday. Maybe it was my pioneer roots, but I always loved the idea of packing up and heading out for a big adventure.

As an adult, I had more freedom to plan camping excursions, but I quickly discovered becoming a real camper takes time. It's a learning process, and one doesn't become experienced overnight. A rainy night in a leaky tent can teach you a thing or two—like it's time to fold your tents and hightail it for home. So camping, like any honed skill, requires practice and patience.

I hope this book will be entertaining—perhaps even inspiring—as I share stories from decades of various forms of camping. Even though I've gone from backpacking to tent camping to owning five very different camp trailers, and, finally, a comfy motor home, I still don't consider myself a seasoned camper. But I'm working on it! Give me a comfortable camp chair, a crackling campfire, a hot cup of coffee, a gooey s'more—and I'm a happy camper.

Here's to you having a memorable camp experience too. Whether you're a weekend warrior or feisty full-timer, I hope you'll be a happy camper too!

Melody Carlson

Entry 1
THE URGE

The mountains are calling and I must go.

JOHN MUIR

You're in your hometown, just going about your business, like mailing a package or picking up some fresh produce, and you see one. You stop and watch from the corner of your eye as a big ol' RV ambles down Main Street. Maybe you admire the paint job, or perhaps you think it's somewhat garish. But that rig's grabbed your attention. Then you wonder: *Where are they headed and where have they been?* And the next thing you know, you have *the urge*—that unexplainable urge to drop everything and hit the road too.

Now you're thinking about the comforting interior of your RV or trailer. Or maybe you're imagining your campsite with that cozy tent all set up and your camp chairs around a crackling fire. You can almost smell marshmallows roasting. You're reminded of the peace and quiet of the woods…and escaping the demands of the day, free from your neighbor's noisy leaf blower.

As you drive through town, you feel an uncontrollable urge to go home and check the air pressure in your camp trailer's tires. Or you want to see if there's gas in the RV. Or you're making plans to dig out your camp supplies, hoping you aired out your tent after that last trip. Whatever the impulse that's grabbing at you, the wanderlust has bitten.

Perhaps you find yourself thinking about that cute set of unbreakable containers you found at the local flea market last fall…or considering the weight of cast-iron pans. And maybe you should drop by the hardware store for some camping toilet paper that's on special this week. Before you know it, you've pulled out your well-worn road map and you're planning a little getaway. Just a few days maybe, or weeks, or months…

But where does that urge originate? Why do some people feel the need to go, while others don't? Could it be the adventuresome spirit of pioneer ancestors, those brave people who traveled unthinkable distances to find a better way of living? Because almost everyone in this country has ancestors who migrated here from someplace else.

No doubt, life on the rustic trail came with daunting challenges, but imagine the moments when a weary traveler paused to gaze upon a raging river, the morning sun across the prairie grasses, a chain of snow-capped mountains, a herd of elk, a placid lake. Despite their hardships, these ultimate campers must have relished the rewards of the wilderness too. Because they had the urge to travel.

Perhaps your ancestors arrived by boat or plane. Whatever brought them to this country, something motivated them to travel. And perhaps that same seed lies within you, a need to go and see, to experience and explore. I think it's simply the way God made some people. We're seekers, hopers, dreamers... curious for what lies over the next hill or what we might find at the end of the rainbow. Any excuse is a good excuse to go.

Wherever this wanderlust comes from, why not simply embrace it? Why not enjoy the thrill of the open highway and head out for your next adventure? Sure, your excursion might last only a day or two, and your biggest thrill might be finding a whole sand dollar on a windswept beach. But when it's all said and done, you'll be happy you went. You'll be a bigger person for it. Maybe you'll even be glad to come back home again. And if not, there's always another unexplored road to find.

It is good to have an end to journey towards;
but it is the journey that matters in the end.

URSULA K. LE GUIN

TIP FOR THE DAY

Resealable plastic bags are perfect for camping. Freezable bags can be filled with soups or stews and frozen at home. Then place them in your cooler to keep other perishable foods cold—and ready for easy eating later. A Ziploc bag filled with premeasured dry ingredients (for your favorite camp recipes) makes cooking quick and easy at camp. Baggies also provide dry protection for matches, first aid items, meds, or whatever.

THE HAVES AND HAVE-NOTS

Money can't buy happiness, but it can buy a camper,
which is kind of the same thing.

AUTHOR UNKNOWN

We're staying at one of the few beachside RV parks in Oregon. On the left side of our trailer is an older Class C motorhome—the kind that looks like a van met a camp trailer and two become one. In this small RV reside *eight* people, including what appear to be grandparents, parents, and kids. I marvel at this extended family's tenacity for surviving in tight spaces, and try not to imagine the smell of those teenage boys' feet on this humid summer day. Although I do wonder where they all sleep. I imagine them stacked head to toe like sardines in a tin.

Suddenly it feels as if our modest although comfortable motor home is quite spacious. And even though our Bounder is getting up there in years, it's in pretty good shape. Not like the crowded one next door. With its faded paint and dents and dings on the outside, I can't imagine what its interior must look like. And each time I hear the door slamming on the little class C, I hope it won't fall off its hinges.

But lest I get smug about our accommodations, I need only look to the right of us to feel like we're the ones slumming. I noticed the fancy RV as soon as it pulled in earlier today. This mobile mansion is shiny and new, and obviously equipped with every convenience imaginable. Custom-designed from a very expensive luxury bus, this huge motor home has an airbrushed mural of a Southwest desert on one side.

It's no secret that these kinds of RVs cost more than most homes and are popular with celebrities and millionaires. Residing inside this palace on wheels is an attractive couple who appear to be in their late fifties. I'm guessing they retired early and are quite well off. Their license plates are from Texas, and I imagine their RV's interior has all the electronic amenities—not to mention dishwasher, washer and dryer, and probably a bathtub to boot. Quite a contrast to the packed-in yet lively neighbors to our left, but that's the way it is in RV parks—the haves and have-nots...and those (like us) somewhere in the middle. But I must admit to being amused by the contrasts.

The big fancy RV is noticeably quiet. I rarely see its owners. Perhaps they're so comfortable inside that they don't care to venture out. Meanwhile, the small rundown motorhome remains lively. People come and go, and we hear snippets of conversation, jovial laughter, and even a few friendly squabbles. But the campers over there seem genuinely happy. They're having fun! It's a good reminder that material wealth or fancy rigs don't guarantee a good time.

A day or two later, I learn that the woman in the luxurious motor home spent the past several years attempting to nurse her adult daughter back to health. But her only child died. The daughter was unmarried and childless… and it seems she took her mother's joy of living with her when she left. The woman's husband tells me this. With hopes of alleviating his wife's grief—and his own—he leased the big fancy motor home for a year. He took a year's leave of absence and set out to see the country. Apparently his plan is starting to work, but they still have a long road ahead of them.

So I am reminded that while one family is out making memories, another is out trying to forget them. The haves and the have-nots.

What a wonderful life I've had!
I only wish I'd realized it sooner.
COLETTE

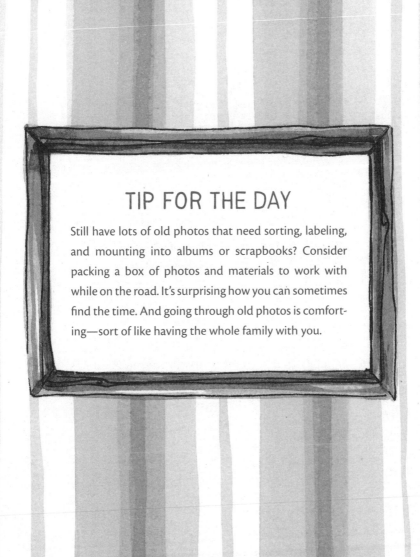

TIP FOR THE DAY

Still have lots of old photos that need sorting, labeling, and mounting into albums or scrapbooks? Consider packing a box of photos and materials to work with while on the road. It's surprising how you can sometimes find the time. And going through old photos is comforting—sort of like having the whole family with you.

A SITE WITH A VIEW

An inconvenience is only
an adventure wrongly considered.

G. K. CHESTERTON

It's midweek in summer when we head up to our favorite mountain lake, secur-ing a secluded campsite with a beautiful view of the placid blue water. Not only do we have our own beach for our kayaks, but it's peaceful and quiet. Until Saturday. Suddenly the campground springs to life with weekenders. Things get noisy, and the Campground Full sign appears.

For some reason, a group of boisterous kids and their colorful parade of inflatable float toys decide to utilize our secluded corner of the lake—as well as "our" beach. Although we see no adults supervising these kids' water activities, a preteen boy in a small kayak appears to be in charge. Even so, I keep an eye on them from my camp chair on the shore, reassuring myself that they're staying relatively safe and hoping I'll remember my lifesaving skills if necessary.

At the end of the day, the older boy herds the kids and all their stuff onto our previously private beach. There, they abandon their bright, oversized fla- mingoes, unicorns, and dragons—heaping their neon menagerie right on top of our kayaks and tying them down so they won't blow or float away. Well, so much for our serene view. The noisy kids take off, but not to any nearby campsite. They seem to just disappear.

Not only has our picturesque beach turned into a kiddy play yard, our kay- aks appear lost in the tangle of discarded toys. My husband, Chris, disgruntled by the mess and attempting to unearth our kayaks, trips over the boy's kayak paddle—and accidentally breaks it. He fiddles with the broken paddle for a bit, but because it's a cheap one, he realizes it can't be fixed. And, he points out, it's the kid's fault since he left it lying in the rubble like that.

That night we turn in early and shortly after sunrise the next morning, my husband makes an excuse to go to town. To my surprise, Chris returns with a nice new paddle and places it in the boy's kayak. By noon, the kids are all back. And the boy, using his new and improved paddle, supervises them once again from his kayak. Whether or not he recognizes the new paddle, we can't be sure. But it's reas- suring to know he has it.

At the end of the day, Chris and I observe the worn-out but happy kids converging in the day-use area. As they load their colorful float toys into the back of an old pickup truck, we visit briefly with their moms. We learn that their moms brought the kids here to enjoy the lake during the daytime hours, but because the campground was full they had to go home at night. They were day-campers, just making the best of it. Tomorrow is a workday for them. The next morning, with our quiet campground, peaceful beach, and pretty view restored to us, I'm surprised to discover that I miss the noisy kids and their colorful toys.

The best and most beautiful things in
this world cannot be seen or even heard,
but must be felt with the heart.

HELEN KELLER

TIP FOR THE DAY

Keep a campground notebook—the kind with folders that can hold campground information such as brochures, flyers, maps, and the like, as well as a space to list your favorite campsite numbers for return visits and important notes and phone numbers.

CAMPFIRE CONNECTIONS

A journey is best measured in friends
rather than miles.

TIM CAHILL

In need of a departure from some life stresses, we eagerly grab the opportunity to get away for a few days of camping. Never mind that the state park campground is only 20 minutes from our home in the nearby town. It feels like a world away. A welcome escape. And although it's summer, by arriving midweek we manage to snag a great camp space.

It doesn't take long to feel relaxed and at home in our rustic campsite. That means it's *dry camping*—which means no water, electric, or any "convenience" hookups. Our fresh water tank is full and the sewage holding tanks are empty. Plus we have a dependable gas stove to cook on, some friendly kerosene lamps, and lots and lots of firewood. There's no cell phone connectivity in the campground, but that's a blessing in disguise, the perfect excuse to completely disconnect and escape for a spell.

After a few days, we've settled into a simple routine of doing little more than sitting in camp chairs and absorbing nature—or staring blankly at nothing in particular. Oh sure, we might take a leisurely walk or read a book—if we feel like it. But the only "labor" is preparing simple food or making a campfire, which feels more like fun than work. We also take time to observe and interact with other campers. To us, that's one of the most important parts of camping. The campers around us are like untold stories, and as a writer, I'm always eager to hear them.

From my campsite, I notice a minivan pulling into a nearby camp space in the late afternoon. With my sunglasses on, I pretend to read, trying to be inconspicuous as I observe the older couple laboriously setting up their campsite. I say *laboriously* because it seems they're doing everything the hard way. They look tired, and, unless I'm imagining it, they seem slightly vexed. I watch as they unload their car, removing cartons and supplies and coolers. The man puts up a tent, and the woman sets up what seems a well-equipped outdoor kitchen—and a lot of work. As they scurry about, getting themselves set up, I start to feel lazy just sitting in my comfy camp chair. And that's when I notice they have no firewood. And evenings have been cool up here in the mountains.

So I decide to go over and offer some of our firewood—since we brought plenty. But when I suggest this to the woman, she crisply tells me *no thanks*. "We're only here for the night," she says in a way that tells me she has no idle time to visit. I don't persist, but as I leave I think it's sad they're going to so much work for just one night—and even sadder that they don't want a campfire.

I relay this to my husband and he, being more persistent, goes back over and not only offers this couple some firewood, but insists on building them a fire. As he builds them this fire, he visits with the man. And that's when everything changes. They invite us to bring our chairs over (after they've finished and cleaned up their dinner). As the sky grows dusky, we bring cocoa and popcorn and more firewood and suddenly we're all sitting around the fire, sharing interesting stories and laughs.

Our newly made friends tell us about how they've spent the last month on a bucket-list item (to visit the Northwest) and tomorrow they will head home to the Midwest. Camping from their car, they've grown weary—but they express sincere gratitude for this evening's campfire and friendship. By the time we call it a night, we feel like old friends and even exchange addresses. A few months later we receive a very sweet thank-you note from this couple. The note says, "That evening was the highlight of our month-long camping trip." All because of a campfire.

No act of kindness, no matter how small, is ever wasted.

AESOP

TIP FOR THE DAY

Keep a camping journal. This not only gives you a way to remember when and where you've camped over the years, but it provides a place to list names of newfound camp friends as well as addresses and phone numbers in case you want to reconnect.

BEST-LAID PLANS

Of all the paths you take in life,
make sure a few of them are dirt.

JOHN MUIR

We're not all natural-born campers. But for some irrational reason, I used to assume that my husband had these hidden talents. I'm not sure why…probably because he was a man, and I figured that's what men did. Also because I knew that he, like me, loved the great outdoors. But what I hadn't realized is that camp savvy, for most people, is probably a learned skill.

So when I decide it's time to take our two boys on a weekend camping trip, I have no idea I will encounter such resistance from their dear old dad. Especially since I handle all the organizing and planning and packing. I reserve the camp spot at a pretty lake. I get the supplies ready. I pack a tent, sleeping bags, and fishing poles, fitting them into the back of our minivan. I get groceries and load the cooler. I tell my boys which clothes to pack.

And on Friday night, when Chris gets home from work, I announce that we're ready to go. He is not enthusiastic, but I imagine that my enthusiasm will make up for it. Or that once we get there, he'll magically transform into a happy camper. Or maybe I'm just delusional. My plan is for the boys and their dad to sleep in the tent, which is supposed to be big enough for four campers, but probably better suited for two. And then I, being the only female, will sleep in the back of the minivan—cramped but not bad. The boys are thrilled with the tent. My husband...not so much.

Still, I try to keep my spirits high as I help set up our camp and start dinner. I suggest Chris go fishing. Trout for dinner sounds good. And perhaps it will improve his general disposition. But when he returns, wet and sore from an unexpected tumble in the creek, his disposition is not improved. And no trout for dinner.

Things aren't better at bedtime. Chris doesn't like sleeping with the boys in the tent. He doesn't like the cheesy air mattresses I got for everyone. He pretty much doesn't like anything, and I wonder if we'll even make it through the night. Somehow we do, but the next morning isn't much better. And eventually I am so fed up with my unhappy camper that I tell him the boys and I will spend the day on our own. He can do as he pleases—without our company.

I have no idea how he spends his free time, but the boys and I enjoy ourselves. We swim and float the lake on our air mattresses. We take a little hike, play games, fix ourselves food, and roast marshmallows. By bedtime, we're tired and dirty and happy. But Chris is still out of sorts.

Somehow we make it through the night. And the next morning, my husband finally steps in to help—to load the van. The only thing he's happy about is going home.

At home, after I unload everything and spend several hours cleaning it all up and putting it away, Chris—after a long nap—sheepishly admits he was simply tired after a long week at work and that his back was aching. By then I'm tired and my back is aching, but I learned a lesson. The best-laid plans of just one person can go sideways. A successful camping trip requires cooperation and communication—from everyone involved.

A bad day camping is still better
than a good day working.
ANONYMOUS

TIP FOR THE DAY

For bare-bones camping, take a pump sprayer filled with water to use for quick cleanups. Good for hands, feet—or a quick shower. Store it in a sunny spot for solar-heated water, or a cool spot if it's a hot day and you need to cool off.

Entry 6
PLAYING HOUSE

I may not have gone where I intended to go,
but I think I have ended up where I intended to be.

DANTE ALIGHIERI

My husband and I eventually conclude that tent camping is not for us. As much as we both love being outdoors and exploring new places, we don't enjoy the work associated with packing all that camp gear, setting up a camp, and then sleeping on a lumpy pad in a damp tent. But perhaps the worst thing, in my opinion, is the necessity to clean, then store, all the messy camp gear after we get home. It's exhausting. I decide we need a camp trailer. And Chris is game.

So we go trailer shopping. Because this will be our first camp trailer, I feel we should be conservative. Nothing too big, too fancy, or too expensive. And, of course, I want it to be attractive. Just because you're camping doesn't mean you should sacrifice style. But keep in mind, this was back in the 1990s, when most camp trailers came in shades of dusty blue and mauve—colors I don't like. And, honestly, unless it's a vintage retro trailer, pink and blue just don't feel campy to me. Why weren't companies making trailers with mossy greens, earthy russets, woodsy tans—colors compatible with the great outdoors? Why would anyone want pink or blue carpet and flowery curtains and wallpaper?

When I finally unearth a small, affordable trailer in pleasant earth tones, I am sold. And Chris, weary of trailer shopping, gladly agrees. We get the trailer, hitch it to his pickup, and head for home. During the 20-minute drive, I feel like a new mother, anxiously looking back to make sure "junior" is still properly connected and traveling smoothly.

At home, I begin to play house inside my new trailer. Naturally, Chris couldn't care less about how I outfit it. Unbeknownst to me, he has another concern brewing. His pickup, which we'd been assured had plenty of horsepower, suddenly doesn't seem strong enough to pull our small trailer. At least to Chris. He's soon looking for a big diesel pickup. Of course, I should've known that any excuse for a bigger truck was a good excuse (in his mind). I honestly wonder if he planned the whole thing from the start.

But I am contentedly playing house in my adorable little trailer. We hope to take it to a big flea market the following weekend, and my goal is to make it so sweet and comfortable that we'll both want to go camping as often as possible. Maybe we'll want to live in it full-time! I get good sheets and towels, cute unbreakable dishware, and other basic necessities. I put in some decorative touches too. Candles, pretty throws and pillows, a few things to hang on the wall, and so on. By the end of the week, our darling little trailer is as cute as can be. She's ready to roll—and Chris's new diesel pickup is ready to pull her. That pickup is so powerful that Chris says he couldn't even feel the trailer behind us as we fly down the highway that day.

Naturally, I'm a little concerned about my sweet little trailer as we travel over the mountain roads. Sure, she looks great on the exterior, but how's she faring inside? After about an hour of driving, I suggest we stop for a few groceries. But when I put the groceries into the trailer, I'm dismayed to discover all is not well. In fact, it's a mess. The motion of traveling knocked pictures off walls. Candles and other unsecured items have tumbled to the floor. A cupboard door not properly latched has even dumped some unbreakable dishes to the floor...and so on.

Another good lesson: Before traveling, make sure everything is secured. I clean up the mess and tuck things in more stable places, wedge them tighter, make sure the hatches are battened, and we head out again. Our final stop is better.

Since that first trailer, I've learned a lot of tricks for securing things. I've also learned it's good to double-check everything before taking off. Make sure all doors, including the fridge, are latched tight. And remember that anything not nailed down, glued down, or wedged down can and will move.

The journey between what you once were and who you are
now becoming is where the dance of life really takes place.
BARBARA DE ANGELIS

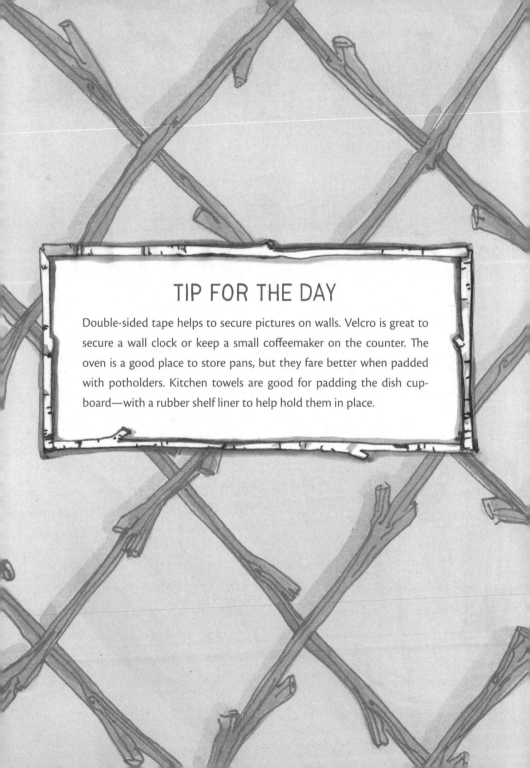

TIP FOR THE DAY

Double-sided tape helps to secure pictures on walls. Velcro is great to secure a wall clock or keep a small coffeemaker on the counter. The oven is a good place to store pans, but they fare better when padded with potholders. Kitchen towels are good for padding the dish cupboard—with a rubber shelf liner to help hold them in place.

GRANDPA'S TRAILER

Twenty years from now, you will be more disappointed
by the things you didn't do than by the ones you did do.
So throw off the bowlines. Sail away from the safe harbor.
Catch the trade winds in your sails.
Explore. Dream. Discover.

ATTRIBUTED TO MARK TWAIN

As the child of a single working mom, the idea of ever going camping in a real camp trailer seems like the impossible dream. Some of our neighbors have trailers, including a gorgeous silver Airstream that Mr. Mitchell keeps polished and gleaming—even though it usually stays in their driveway. I peek inside that trailer once, and marvel at how nice it is, wishing we could have one too. But my mom points out that our neighbors are "well off." And we are not.

During this era, I spend most of my summers and holidays at my grandparents' house. My grandfather is a skilled woodworker. After retiring, he builds several impressive boats for other people, including a cabin cruiser with sleeping quarters. I am so impressed, convinced my clever grandpa can build anything.

I love watching Grandpa in his workshop, and I probably mention my trailer fancies to him…but when he starts creating a camp trailer I am all in. I observe with fascination as he constructs the trailer's framework, shaping the wood into curves. Then he uses plywood for the outer shell, even putting in real windows. Finally, he covers it in shiny aluminum metal, like Mr. Mitchell's, only smaller. Next, Grandpa goes to work on the compact interior. He uses smooth, finish-grade plywood for walls. He makes a tiny kitchenette, complete with cabinets, a little plumbed sink, and a two-burner gas stove. He makes a banquet table that magically transforms into a bed, then adds another bigger bed in back. He even makes a tiny closet that's big enough to hold the porta potty my grandma insists is a necessity. Really, what more could you want?

After my grandpa's carpentry work is done, my grandma steps in. She brings fabrics and her sewing machine to the trailer. She upholsters the banquette's benches. Then, sitting at the banquette table, she sews sweet little curtains for the windows. After that, she furnishes the trailer with kitchen items, bedding, and even a small braided rug that she made. The final results are truly delightful. And I'm so proud that my grandparents made it themselves. I love that trailer so much that I would like to live in it—and I can't wait to go camping in it.

And I get to go on numerous memorable camping trips with my grandparents.

Looking back, I realize their trailer was pretty tiny, but it didn't feel overly small back then. In fact, it felt perfect. And I know that little trailer planted seeds in me…making me look forward to the day when I would get my own trailer.

Even now, five trailers and one motor home later, I can still feel my grandparents' influence. And although we haven't actually built our own trailer, I did get to restore a vintage trailer, which was almost like building it. And, like my grandma, I've often taken my sewing machine out to a trailer or motor home to sew curtains or do some reupholstering. And it never fails that, while engrossed in any of my various trailer projects, I am reminded of my grandparents' can-do spirit—and their love of camping. And I am grateful.

Oh, the places you'll go.

DR. SEUSS

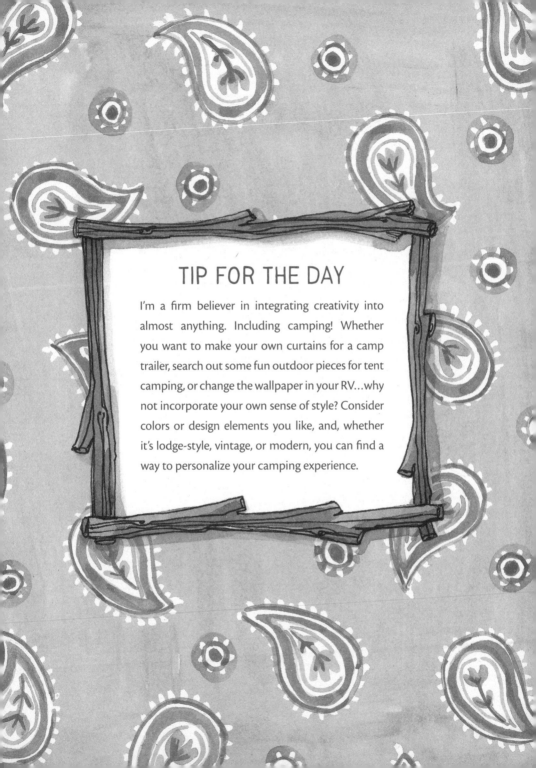

TIP FOR THE DAY

I'm a firm believer in integrating creativity into almost anything. Including camping! Whether you want to make your own curtains for a camp trailer, search out some fun outdoor pieces for tent camping, or change the wallpaper in your RV...why not incorporate your own sense of style? Consider colors or design elements you like, and, whether it's lodge-style, vintage, or modern, you can find a way to personalize your camping experience.

Entry 8

SLEEPAWAY CAMP

Adventure is a path.
Real adventure, self-determined, self-motivated,
often risky, forces you to have
firsthand encounters with the world.

MARK JENKINS

Do you remember your first overnight camping experience? Although I have fond memories of camping with my grandparents, going to sleepover camp stands out in my memory as one of my first camping adventures. Probably because it was something I did completely on my own.

I am only ten when I convince my mother I'm old enough to handle a week of sleepover camp. Never mind that my older sister has no interest in such endeavors, and none of my friends are going. I eagerly go over the camp list, crossing off each item as I collect it. I never had a waterproof soapbox before, and I wonder why I need a "personal" towel and washcloth. I still remember the musty canvas smell of the army surplus store—where I go to get a duffel bag and sleeping bag. We're allowed only one duffel bag, so I must stuff my sleeping bag into the bottom, leaving about ten inches to cram in the rest of my belongings. But being a tomboy ten-year-old, there's not much to pack.

Despite my independent bravado, telling my mom and sister they don't need to hang around to say goodbye, I feel nervous as I wait for the camp bus to show up at the city park. And when I see other families seeing off their kids, many who are older than I am, I feel a little strange. As they exchange hugs and kisses, I notice a few curious looks: Do they think I'm an orphan or something?

But I keep my chin up and load my duffel bag onto the back of the bus, acting like I'm an old hand at this. By the time we're all loaded onto the bus and the leaders start leading camp songs like "The Ants Go Marching," I gladly join in.

I love the feeling of going somewhere exciting. And when we get to Camp Silver Falls, I feel like I've come home. Okay, a home away from home. I love the smell of the pine trees, the look of the big lodge, and the little wood cabins with bunk beds not so different from mine at home. I love the lake with its long dock and colorful canoes. I love everything. I am a natural-born camper.

A few other girls in my cabin—even ones with friends here—get homesick. But not me. It's not that I don't love my mom and sis; I just don't really miss them much. But I do write a postcard or two. And even though I like to write, I keep my reports brief. There's too much to do here. Canoeing, swimming, sports, the craft shed, archery…there aren't enough hours in the day to do it all!

The food is okay, but my favorite meal is when we make hobo stew in the campfire coals. And I love the end of the day when all the campers gather around a giant campfire…and the singing and the ghost stories and making s'mores.

I've heard that if you want to discover what you'd like to be as an adult, you should remember what you loved as a ten-year-old. Well, I can admit I loved writing, but I also loved camping. I guess that explains a few things.

> We shall not cease from exploration
> And the end of all our exploring
> Will be to arrive where we started
> And know the place for the first time.
>
> T.S. ELIOT

TIP FOR THE DAY

When preparing for camping, I try to remember that, as a ten-year-old, I didn't need that many clothes to get by. Really, less is more. Traveling light makes sense with camping. Remember to pack—and to dress—in layers. Choose fabrics and styles that are comfortable—and make you feel good. Have something for all temperatures, whether it's the crisp chill of morning, the sun-baking heat of day, or protecting yourself from mosquitoes in the evening.

REALLY SIMPLE HOBO STEW
(aka Mulligan Stew)

1 sweet onion, chopped

2 T. olive oil

1 lb. stew meat chunks (or 1 lb. hamburger)

1 tsp. seasoning (I use Montreal steak seasoning)

Salt and pepper

1 (14.5 oz.) can diced tomatoes

1 small bag baby carrots

1 small bag baby potatoes

Other veggies you like (corn, celery, mushrooms)

2 (14.5 oz.) cans beef broth

Sauté the onion in the olive oil (or, if you like bacon, you can chop up some and sauté the onions with it). Add the meat and brown. Add the seasoning and salt and pepper to taste, and then transfer the meat and onion mixture to a Crock-Pot or Dutch oven. Add the veggies and broth, and slow cook in the Crock-Pot for six to ten hours. Or you can cook on the stove or over an open fire until the potatoes are tender.

Serves 4 to 6 with leftovers.

Entry 9
SIZE MATTERS

Life is 10 percent what happens to you,
and 90 percent how you react to it.

CHARLES R. SWINDOLL

As much as I love our first trailer—the small, affordable one with the attractive color scheme, I soon discover that my sweet little trailer has a fatal flaw. Something both my husband and I never noticed when purchasing it; something that becomes very difficult to live with. Even for a weekend.

It's embarrassing to admit to our ignorance now, but I know that many first-time trailer buyers make similar mistakes. In our enthusiasm and inexperience, we sometimes overlook a few things. Some things are fixable. Some things not so much. For instance, there's little you can do about an awkward floor plan, a bathroom that's too small, an inconvenient kitchen, or a bed that's too small. And those things can take some of the fun out of camping.

So we're on our first camping trip. Our little trailer, pulled by the heavy-duty diesel pickup, arrives in one piece. We meet up with some family and friends and get settled into a rustic camping area outside of a fun flea market in a remote small town. Because it's late in the day, we get settled outside around a campfire and enjoy visiting until it's time for bed. I can't wait for our first night in our sweet little trailer. Although the queen-sized bed will be an adjustment from our king at home, I think it'll be cozy and comfortable. And I will not complain if Chris takes more than his half of it.

Everything about our little trailer, in my opinion, is perfect. And I'm as happy as a clam. Fortunately, we're both tired enough that we enjoy a fairly decent night's sleep. Then we join the others outside for breakfast, sitting in camp chairs, sipping coffee, and making plans for the flea market.

It's not until after a long day of "treasure hunting" that I notice Chris is walking funny. Kind of crooked. But I realize he walks like that only *inside* our trailer. At first I think his bad back must be bothering him again. It's an ongoing condition that we've learned to live with. But suddenly, I realize it's something else entirely.

You see, Chris is a tall guy. Nearly a foot taller than I. He's six feet and six inches tall—and the ceiling of our little trailer is only six feet four inches high. You get the picture. The poor man can't stand up straight. After I recover from the shock, I can't help but see the humor. Seriously, what were we think-ing? The question is...*what now?*

Chris assures me that we can make it

work. "I mostly sit or sleep when I'm in the trailer anyway," he says. But I'm not so sure. And I feel incredibly stupid for having overlooked this when we bought our trailer. Good grief, was I so focused on color schemes that I completely missed something this important? Of course, I remind myself, Chris missed it too. And it's his head that's bent like that. But he continues to act like it's no big deal.

So we take our little trailer on a few more outings, and, despite my husband's optimism that he can make it work, I am not convinced. And after he almost knocks himself out going through the bedroom or bathroom doorway a few times—sometimes in the middle of the night—I realize this trailer is a mistake. As much as I love my sweet little trailer, I love my husband more! Somehow, I'll figure a way out of this predicament.

All you need to know is that it's possible.
WOLF, AN APPALACHIAN TRAIL HIKER

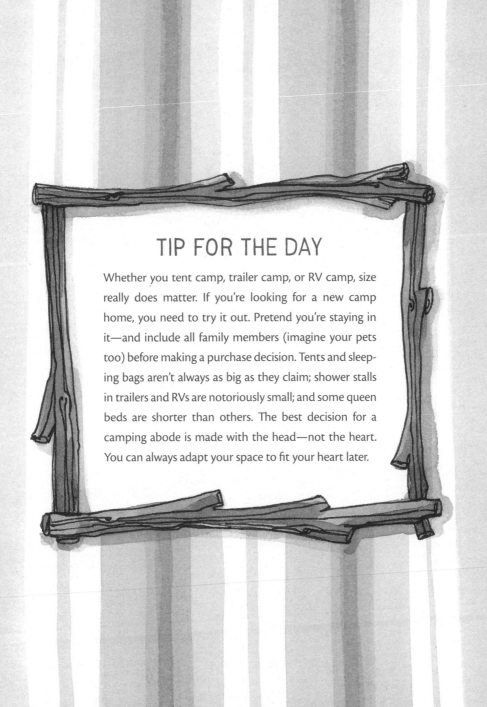

TIP FOR THE DAY

Whether you tent camp, trailer camp, or RV camp, size really does matter. If you're looking for a new camp home, you need to try it out. Pretend you're staying in it—and include all family members (imagine your pets too) before making a purchase decision. Tents and sleeping bags aren't always as big as they claim; shower stalls in trailers and RVs are notoriously small; and some queen beds are shorter than others. The best decision for a camping abode is made with the head—not the heart. You can always adapt your space to fit your heart later.

Entry 10
CAMP FOOD

Wilderness is not a luxury but a necessity of the human spirit.

EDWARD ABBEY

One of my favorite childhood campouts was the time my sister and I camped at the beach with our grandparents. Both my grandparents were from pioneer stock—and that is exactly the term they used to describe it when they'd explain how their families had come to Oregon via covered wagons. My grandpa's ancestors came by wagon train across the Oregon Trail in the early 1850s, and my grandmother's family traveled through the Southwest in a covered wagon in the early 1900s. Suffice it to say, my grandparents both had pioneering in their blood. I suppose I like to think I got some of that from them.

So my sister and I are camping along the Oregon coast with Grandma and Grandpa. And even though my sis has never been much of an outdoor girl, she seems to enjoy exploring the campground with me. We shell-hunt along the beach, roll down the sand dunes, play cards with Grandma, and help her with camp cooking. Grandma is a good cook—and although I'm a picky eater, she always entices me to try new things. Like sardines. Now you wouldn't think a kid, especially a picky eater, would like those greasy, smelly fishes. But when Grandma demonstrates how to eat them on saltine crackers, I'm hooked. And Grandma even knows how to make saltwater taffy.

One of my favorite meals in that little camp trailer is when Grandpa brings home some crabs. Grandma cooks them in a big pot over the campfire outside the trailer, and then we all sit around the banquet table, which is covered with newspapers. Aided by hammers and pliers, we hack into those crabs and devour every piece. I never knew I loved crab, but that night I discover it's delicious!

Another staple of camp food is Mulligan Stew. No one makes it like Grandma. She uses bacon and onions and whatever else is handy. Then she lets it simmer for a good long time...so the flavor of meat, potatoes, carrots, and tomatoes get mingled just right.

But the best camp eating ever happens when my sister and I discover clams on the beach. We notice someone digging with a shovel and watch as he removes a clam. Curious as to whether we can do the same, we get down on our hands and knees and dig eagerly. To our astonishment, we find clams. Nice big clams. And lots of them. Without a bucket, we load the clams into our T-shirts and run them back to the campsite, proudly displaying our find. Grandma is as thrilled as we are. She gives us plastic bread bags and says, "Go get more."

And we do! Feeling like real pioneers, we return to camp with bread sacks heavy with clams. Grandma puts the clams in a big bucket of water, then sprinkles in cornmeal, explaining the clams will "eat" the cornmeal, which helps to clean them. That night, Grandma fries up big clam fritters—which are delicious. The next day we have creamy clam chowder.

No one made chowder like Grandma. Maybe because her family was from North Carolina. Fortunately, I still have her recipe, and it's one of my favorite soups—both at home and on the road.

Who has smelled the wood-smoke at twilight,
Who has seen the campfire burning,
Who is quick to read the noises of the night?
RUDYARD KIPLING

TIP FOR THE DAY

Minimal necessities for campfire cooking:

> aluminum foil

> fire-starter material

> firewood

> matches and lighter fluid

> medium to large pot, frying pan, and lid

> portable grate to place over a fire pit

> salt and pepper

> spatula, tongs, and oversized spoon

EASY BREEZY CLAM CHOWDER

Several strips of bacon, cut in small pieces

1 sweet onion, chopped

1 lb. potatoes, chopped (I use small golden Yukons)

5 (6.5 oz.) cans chopped clams (drain the juice but
   save it for the chowder)

1 tsp. seasoning (I like Old Bay)

3 cups whole milk

In a large pot, sauté the bacon and onion together. When cooked, add the potatoes, the juice from the clams, and the seasoning. Add enough water to cover the potatoes and simmer for 20 minutes. Then add the clams and the milk and bring back to a simmer. Cook for 10 more minutes.

Serves 4 to 6.

PACKING IN

Life is either a daring adventure or nothing.

HELEN KELLER

Camping can bring out the best and the worst in a person. And backpacking… probably even more so! Being young and naïve, I think the idea of taking a bunch of teens on a weekend backpacking trip sounds adventurous. It might even be fun. And because my fiancé (Chris) and I are youth leaders, I figure it's up to us and the other two leaders to set a good example for the teens. But let me state, here and now, that it was the guy leaders' idea to take this trip.

I was well aware that some of these high school girls weren't the least bit campy. They were the kind of girls who'd complain over a broken nail or frizzed hair. Still, I thought the girls and I could have a good time. I could imagine us cooking food together, bonding around the campfire, stargazing, sharing secrets in the privacy of our tent at night. It could work.

Because of our jobs, Chris and I arrive late to the trailhead. We're aware that the other leaders will leave some supplies for us to pack in. But judging by the huge pile of food sitting in our friend's pickup, the others couldn't have carried much. Although Chris loads lots of food items in his pack, plenty of heavy cans are packed into mine.

My pack grows so heavy that I can barely lift it. Chris helps me put it on, but if I lean backward, even just slightly, I'll be toast. Still, I don't want to complain. I don't know how far we must go to reach the high mountain lake where the others are waiting, but I think I can tough it out. As we hike in, my pack feels heavier and heavier. I keep wondering why the others didn't pack some of these supplies in. But when the sun goes down, and we're stumbling through the darkness, tripping over rocks and tree roots (and my pack feels heavier than ever), I'm trying not to get mad. I pray to make it in one piece, and I'm determined not to complain.

Finally we reach camp with what turns out to be *all of the food*. Everyone thinks it's a great joke that we got stuck lugging it all in. As Chris helps me remove my pack, he's surprised at how heavy it is. He apologizes for not putting more of the canned goods in his pack. Still, I don't complain. I'm just relieved to be here. We fix dinner and have a good campfire that evening. And although some of the high school kids start whining about the cool weather and deprivations of camping, I try to keep my attitude positive. Chris does too.

The next day, we wake to cold misty weather that dampens my spirits, but I try not to show it.

Instead, we keep things fun and lively as we encourage the kids to participate in the camp chores. We decide to keep our campfire burning all day, which means we need more firewood. Chris takes charge of this, but after a while he cuts his hand on the ax. I help him bandage it, hoping he doesn't need stitches. I'm relieved that he doesn't complain.

By late afternoon, it starts raining hard, and I bite my tongue, determined not to chime in with the girls who are loudly complaining about being wet and cold and sick of camping in the mud. I wouldn't mind pulling the plug on this trip, but I'm not going there. Somehow we make it through the miserable night and wake to sunshine the next morning. We lay out wet clothes and camp things to dry in the sun, but we are a sorry-looking, bedraggled bunch. Everyone is worn-out and dirty. Even the counselors' attitudes have deteriorated.

That's when I notice that Chris, despite his wounded hand and aching back (from doing more than his fair share of chores), hasn't complained once. And, sure, I haven't either—*not audibly*—but I'm growling beneath the skin and can't wait to get out of here. I want to go home and take a hot bath. But as we hike out, with lighter packs, I realize that I'm engaged to a good man. And that makes up for the weekend's discomforts.

If you can survive camping with someone,
you should marry them on the way home.
YVONNE PRINZ

TIP FOR THE DAY

The basic elements of a wilderness campfire are simple. But before striking a match, be sure campfires are allowed. You need: tinder—that's twigs, dry leaves, pine needles; kindling of small, dry sticks; and firewood, which can be gathered from fallen trees and limbs. You also need a sharp ax (handled carefully) or a small saw, and matches.

If you don't have a fire ring, make your own with rocks. You also need a shovel and water bucket to extinguish your fire. The best wilderness campfire builders "leave no trace."

Entry 12

MOVING UP

I just want to live in a world of mountains,
coffee, campfires, cabins, and golden trees,
and run around with a camera and notebook,
learning the inner workings of everything real.

AUTHOR UNKNOWN

It doesn't take too many camping trips before my husband and I both decide we need a bigger trailer—specifically one with a higher ceiling. This time I let Chris take the lead. Impressed with four-season trailers that fare well in the cold temps, which we get in the mountains, he opts for an Arctic Fox. Fortunately, their ceilings are taller than he is. And the RV place gives us a good trade-in for our barely used little trailer.

When you're married to an oversized man, you get used to living in and among big things. Whether it's furniture, vehicles, or sports equipment, we've learned to supersize. And the trailer Chris picks is definitely big. About 30 feet long, with three slide-outs. Compared to our starter trailer, this new trailer feels like a mansion. I think we could live in it if we wanted.

Thanks to the way Chris already supersized his pickup, there's no trouble in hauling this much heavier trailer. As we take it home, I must admit that it looks handsome behind our pickup. But I still have a feeling it's a little too big. And I'm not in love with the interior decor. At least it's not pink and blue. In fact, it's just the opposite. I'm sure it was designed to appeal to a *man's man*, because all the upholstery fabric looks like camouflage. "Hunters love this trailer," the salesman informs us. But I make it clear to Chris that this is not going to be a hunting trailer. I've seen those trailers. They get used and abused and usually smell like dirty socks.

As Chris parks our big trailer at home, backing it into our designated spot, I start concocting a plan to soften up this overly masculine trailer. Before long I'm taking measurements and making notes. Then it's off to the fabric store. My plan isn't to turn it into a girlie trailer—that would be silly. Instead, my goal is a compromise that will be aesthetically pleasing to both of us. Fortunately, the fabric choices offer some great options. By the next day, I have my sewing machine set up inside the trailer—just like my grandma did when I was a girl. And with coordinated upholstery fabrics that would look great in a mountain lodge, I go to work.

It takes a couple of days to re-cover the banquette benches and couch, as well as the fabric valances, but the results are well worth it. It's perfect. To go along with my lodge theme, I find a wallpaper border featuring moose and lakes and cabins. I use it to replace the black and beige camouflage border, which I eagerly strip off. I also find some cute accessories with moose and bear, and by the end of the week my lodge-style trailer is set. The camouflage is a thing of the past, and I can't wait to go camping.

Okay, I still have the underlying feeling that this trailer is too big for us, but I admit that it's very comfortable. And Chris, who fully approves my decor choices, is one happy camper. Soon, we're planning to meet up with family and friends for a camping weekend. I'm curious about what they'll think of our big new trailer. But if we have bad weather, which often happens in Oregon, we can offer everyone a roomy space to gather, protected from the rain and cold. Still, I wonder...how big is *too* big?

I go to nature to be soothed and healed,
and to have my senses put in order.

JOHN BURROUGHS

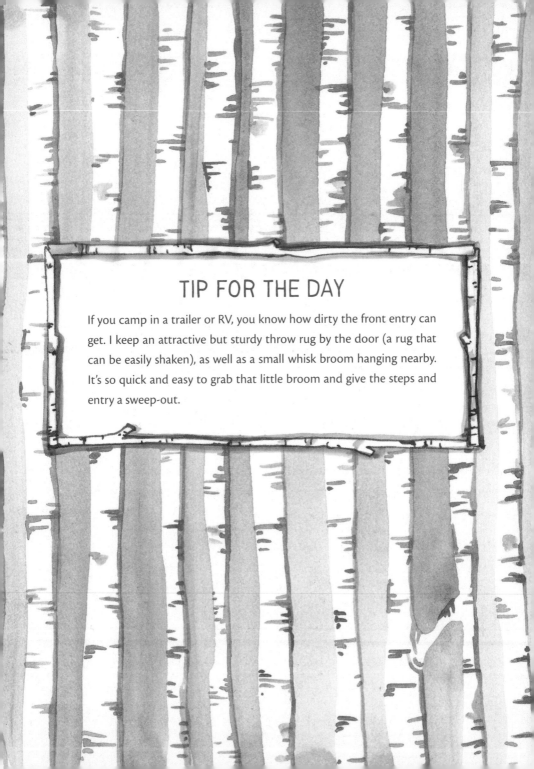

TIP FOR THE DAY

If you camp in a trailer or RV, you know how dirty the front entry can get. I keep an attractive but sturdy throw rug by the door (a rug that can be easily shaken), as well as a small whisk broom hanging nearby. It's so quick and easy to grab that little broom and give the steps and entry a sweep-out.

Entry 13
THE LONG, LONG TRAILER

The life you have led doesn't need to be
the only life you have.

ANNA QUINDLEN

So, we're happy campers as we haul our new Arctic Fox trailer to its first real campout. The diesel pickup has no problem pulling the heavier trailer, but I notice that, when we get gas, then stop for groceries, it's tricky to maneuver or park our rather large trailer. It's about 12 feet longer than our previous trailer. That's a big difference.

I remind myself that it's not nearly as long as the trailer in the classic film with Lucille Ball and Desi Arnaz. As much as I love *The Long, Long Trailer* movie, I cringe to think of those mountain scenes where their lives were in peril because of their oversized trailer. But we're not going down any dangerously narrow mountain roads today. And our pickup is powerful enough to handle this trailer.

When we arrive at our destination, Chris lets me out so I can go figure out where we're supposed to meet up with our family and friends, who are already camped there. It's another big flea market in an old gold-mining town, and somehow they've reserved a large lot that's big enough for all our trailers. This is before cell phones had good connectivity in remote areas, so Chris and I have gone old-school by using a set of miniature walkie-talkies to communicate. I soon find the lot and the other campers and let Chris know where we are. But as I look at the modest and older trailers that are circled around, like an old-fashioned wagon train, I realize the space left for us is rather small. I remember that no one here knows we have a bigger trailer.

Suddenly I feel like we really are reenacting a scene from that old Lucy and Desi movie, as I try to direct Chris—aided by a few "helpful" others—in backing our very long trailer into an awkward and possibly too-small space. Naturally, there's some good-natured ribbing going on, but I can see Chris's frustrations rising as he tries again and again to fit our trailer into the tight spot. It's not easy. We're not even sure it's possible.

After what seems like hours (and way too much stress), the trailer is finally parked. Not nice and neat, like the other much smaller trailers, but sort of cock-eyed and crooked. It looks like a goofy Great Dane who's bedded down with a cute litter of beagle pups. As we stabilize our trailer and set up camp, the teasing con-tinues. Even more so when we deploy the three slide-outs.

"Where'd you get that Taj Mahal?"

"Is that a trailer or a hotel?"

It's mostly the men who are making the comments.

I try to take it in stride, joking back at them. I explain that I'm married to a supersized guy and that we needed more room. I tell them about how our other trailer was too short—and they laugh. But I am feeling embarrassed. Like this trailer is really too much. Oh, sure it's comfortable and nice, but it feels over the top.

It's not long before the women, curious about our long, long trailer, ask to see more of it. Of course, I welcome them inside and, of course, they're stunned at how big it is. They can't believe the size of the kitchen, the spacious bathroom, that it has two TVs and a back door in the bedroom. I try to make light of it, but I'm feeling embarrassed. Who really needs this much trailer? Just for camping?

But with room for everyone, we all sit in there comfortably visiting, and I offer the women snacks. Before long they all agree that it's a nice trailer. We wind up having a good weekend, and Chris and I both feel relaxed and refreshed when it's time to go home. We've enjoyed the comforts of our long, long trailer.

And there is the most dangerous risk of all—
the risk of spending your life not doing what you want
on the bet you can buy yourself the freedom to do it later.

RANDY KOMISAR

TIP FOR THE DAY

If you like to use a variety of spices when you cook but don't want to bring full containers, consider using old Tic Tac boxes. Peel off the label, fill the boxes, write the spices' names on the white (easy-to-open) lid, and you're all set.

Entry 14

MORE IS MORE

People don't take trips, trips take people.

JOHN STEINBECK

I feel honored when I get to accompany my grandparents on a special camping trip. It's my first time to camp in their relatively new trailer. Our destination is a good fishing lake about three hours away. And my grandpa has a brand-new car to pull the homemade trailer. Grandma's brother is the dealer who sold them this flashy red and white Rambler, assuring them that the high-powered engine can pull the lightweight trailer anywhere.

We leave early in the morning and, as usual, I sit between my grandparents in the front seat because of my tendency to get carsick. Especially on winding roads like this. Grandma is sure that if I can see the road ahead of me, I won't lose my breakfast. As usual, she is right. Our trip is uneventful, and I'm not the least bit carsick.

We reach the lake before noon and set up camp. As always, I'm impressed with my grandparents' resourcefulness. Whether it's using a sock to store a bar of soap, or a metal coat hanger to secure a cooking pot, or always having hot water on the fire, ready for washing hands or dishes, they seem to know all the best camping tricks.

For the next few days we enjoy gorgeous summer weather, the company of our other relatives, good fishing, lake swimming, campfire gatherings, and more. Then it's time to go home. After we spend the morning packing up camp, we say goodbye to our relatives and head for my grandparents' home. It's a hot day and, although the new car has air-conditioning, I notice that Grandpa's not using it. Grandma notices this too. Sounding a bit aggravated, she points it out.

"Open your window," Grandpa tells us in a slightly terse tone.

Grandma opens her window, but the air outside feels hot too. She voices this to my grandpa, and he tells her he'll turn on the vents. She questions how this is going to help, but he seems adamantly opposed to using the air conditioner.

Suddenly, hot air pours into the car, and I'm sitting right where it seems to be coming from. I have no idea what the temperature is, but I feel like a cookie in an Easy-Bake Oven. And my grandma can't take anymore. "Pull over," she tells Grandpa in an irate voice I've never heard her use.

Grandpa finds a pullout area, and Grandma and I get out of the hot car. She tells me to sit on a log in the shade. Then she gets something from the trailer and returns to join me. In her hand is a pickle jar that she seems to have filled with water. She dips her hand-kerchief into it and dabs us both with her pickle-water juice. Although the water is cool, it smells like pickles. Then, even though we're sitting in plain sight of the road, Grandma unbuttons her blouse and douses herself with more pickle-water. I'm only about eight, but I'm embarrassed to see my grandma partially undressed and pouring pickle-water down her chest. But I keep my thoughts to myself.

In the meantime, I see Grandpa carrying water to the front of the car and doing something under the hood. Later, he admits to us that the car's overheating—and he's been running the heater to cool it off. No wonder we felt cooked. We make several stops to cool off and refill the radiator. And after we get home, Grandpa takes what Grandma is now calling the Tomato Soup Can back to her brother and exchanges it for a better car.

Traveling—it leaves you speechless,
then turns you into a storyteller.
IBN BATTUTA

TIP FOR THE DAY

Whether it's a tent-trailer, teardrop trailer, or the long, long trailer, you need a vehicle with *more* than enough power and weight to haul it. Manufacturers' listed "trailer weights" can be misleading. You need to plan for a fully loaded trailer. This means more than your cast-iron pans and cowboy boots. Factor in all the holding tanks too—and remember that liquids are heavy. So keep this in mind: When it comes to tow-vehicle engines, *more really is more.*

BUFFALO BINGE

The road of life twists and turns
and no two directions are ever the same.
DON WILLIAMS JR.

My husband has always held a fascination with buffalo and, according to him, buffalo (aka bison) have an affinity for him too. I've heard his boyhood "buffalo survival" story many times. He claims he was charged by a huge wooly beast with only a flimsy chain-link fence between them. According to his older sisters, Chris was teasing the poor buffalo by shaking the fence—and perhaps saying something offensive in bison-ese.

Anyway, on our trip to Yellowstone National Park we are both looking forward to seeing lots of wildlife. I'm probably more excited about moose than buffalo because I've never seen a real live moose. But after settling into camp, we tour around the huge park and I quickly discover that moose sightings are rare right now. Meanwhile, the buffalo seem to be everywhere.

Traffic on the park road is often stopped for buffalo crossing. But it's fun to watch—from the safety of our pickup—the big hairy beasts lumbering along. Naturally Chris wants to get closer, but I'm comfortable keeping a safe distance. Some drivers don't seem too patient and one even honks a horn, which seems ridiculous. If they didn't want to see wildlife, why did they come here? Eventually the bison move along and we do too. But still no moose.

We eventually learn that the bison herd is so big this year that a park ranger is holding a special meeting for our campground. He warns us that the herds are frequently coming through this area—not far from where our trailer is parked. He gives all the campers specific instructions on what to do and not to do. It seems pretty basic—just common sense—but I'm glad Chris has to hear it.

The ranger explains that bison have injured and killed more people in Yellowstone than any other animal in the park. Even grizzlies. "Just because a fuzzy bison might look friendly doesn't mean it is," he says. He also tells us that bison can run three times faster than humans: "So keep a distance. At least 25 yards."

Of course, as soon as the ranger's speech is done, Chris wants to go over to the area where the herd will soon be passing through. Although we watch from a safe distance, I calculate that I probably can't run as fast as the average person. What if a buffalo runs four times faster than I do? Fortunately no one is attacked or trampled.

By the time we're heading for the lodge and geyser area, I'm feeling more at ease with the buffalo, which seem to be everywhere. Still, I'm mindful of keeping a safe distance. We watch Old Faithful spout and then spend time in the lodge, getting lots of good photos of everything. As we're leaving the lodge via a back door, I notice a handsome statue of a huge buffalo right next to the lodge. Thinking this is a good photo-moment, I ask Chris to stand by the very realistic sculpture. But as we get nearer, we notice that the "statue" moves. It's a live buffalo! And only a few feet away. I hear him huff, and I think I can even smell him.

We cautiously back off and then hurry back inside, where we mention this anomaly to an employee, inquiring if anyone is in danger or if they should block the back door. The guy just shrugs like it's no big deal: "Yeah, they come here all the time to eat the soft green grass that grows under the awnings."

We get some photos of the lodge buffalo and continue on our way. Of course, Chris thinks this is the best thing ever. But I'm still hoping to spot a moose. On our way out of Yellowstone, I do see some moose...from a distance. And I hate to admit it, but they are not as exciting as the buffalo.

We live in a wonderful world
that is full of beauty, charm and adventure.
There is no end to the adventures we can have
if only we seek them with our eyes open.
JAWAHARIAL NEHRU

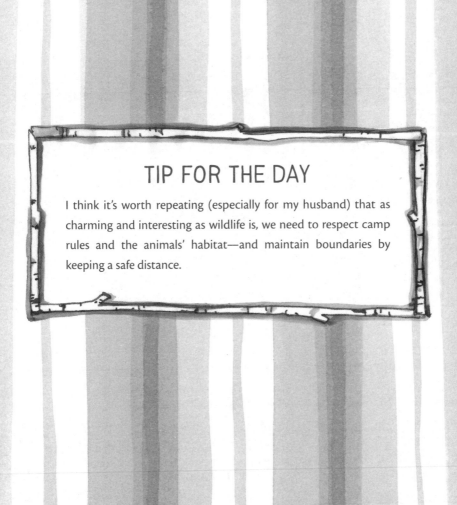

TIP FOR THE DAY

I think it's worth repeating (especially for my husband) that as charming and interesting as wildlife is, we need to respect camp rules and the animals' habitat—and maintain boundaries by keeping a safe distance.

THE WORST CAMPING TRIP EVER

There's a time to persevere and a time to let go.
Your ability to know the difference
will be your greatest source of strength.

DR. ALAN GOLDBERG

As much as I love the overall camping experience, I must admit there's one particular campout that I've tried to forget. In fact, if my husband hadn't recently reminded me, it would probably still be buried somewhere in the back of my brain.

It's early summer and I am pregnant with our first child. Very pregnant—the baby is due in July. Even so, it doesn't occur to me that it might not be the best idea to go camping out in the wilderness. And remember, this is before cell phones. *It's only for a weekend*, I tell myself as we're driving into the mountains. And our friends have already started to set up camp. Besides, I remind myself, this might be my last chance to go camping for a while. Never mind that the weather is overcast, or that we'll be camping in a tent. It'll be fun to meet up with our friends.

And it is fun, at first. The campground is charming. We have a good site to set up our tent. And, because I'm pregnant, Chris doesn't even expect me to help—and I don't. But our other friends (none who have children or have been pregnant) seem to be under the impression that I can still do the things we used to do. Content to be a bystander, I decline to play softball or tag football. Too bad no one brought horseshoes.

As the day progresses, the weather declines. By dinnertime it's a steady drizzle. But we make the best of it, hunkering beneath a tarp awning to eat, playing cards and nursing a sickly campfire. But by the time the sun sets, the rain is really coming down. Chris and I call it a night and, excusing ourselves into our chilly, damp tent, we crawl into our down sleeping bags and hope the deluge will let up before our tent starts to leak. Tomorrow will be a new day. Hopefully a sunny one. We can tough it out.

Assuming that Chris is happy to be here with our friends, I keep my pity party to myself and try to get comfortable, but I am so miserable that I can barely stand it. Being eight months pregnant makes sleeping a challenge in the first place, but in a soggy tent with a lumpy floor? It's impossible. Still, I'm determined to gut it out. After all, it's the middle of the night. What choice do I have?

It's close to midnight when Chris asks if I'm awake. "Of course I'm awake," I tell him, blinking back tears. Then he asks if I'm *okay*. Unable to hold back, I confess that I'm freezing, and the baby is kicking, and I cannot sleep. "I hate this," I say.

"Let's go," he declares.

"Right now? In the middle of the night?"

"Yep." He helps me out of my bag, and as I get fully dressed, he gathers our sleeping bags. I'm concerned we might disturb the others, but no one seems to be awake as we slip out of our tent. The rain is still coming down hard as Chris, carrying a load of stuff, walks me to the pickup. He starts the engine and turns on the heat before heading back to camp for our tent and gear. As I sit there waiting, glad to be in a dry place and hoping to get warm, I feel slightly guilty. Have I ruined Chris's weekend? And I can just imagine the ribbing we'll take from our friends for folding our tent and running home.

When Chris returns with our soggy (unfolded) tent, he tells me that no one even noticed our hasty exodus. By now the pickup is warm. As we drive home, we chuckle over how our friends will react. Maybe they'll think we've been abducted by aliens—or raptured to heaven and they got left behind. But we don't really care—we just want to get home to our warm apartment, a soft bed, and some real rest.

The next afternoon, one of our friends calls to check on us. They did wonder about our welfare. Some speculated I went into labor. Then our friend admits they had a horrible, sleepless night with leaking tents. They woke to a flooded campground—and more rain. They abandoned camp before breakfast.

Chris later confides to me that he was as eager to leave as I was—maybe more so—and grateful I provided him a good excuse. We decide that it's good to know when to cut your losses, fold your tents, and head for higher ground.

You build on failure.
You use it as a stepping stone.
Close the door on the past.
You don't try to forget the mistakes,
but you don't dwell on it.
You don't let it have any of your energy,
or any of your time, or any of your space.

JOHNNY CASH

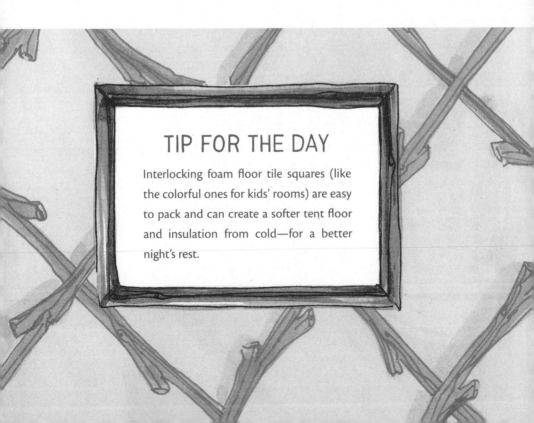

TIP FOR THE DAY

Interlocking foam floor tile squares (like
the colorful ones for kids' rooms) are easy
to pack and can create a softer tent floor
and insulation from cold—for a better
night's rest.

Entry 17

CAMPING WITH TEENS

Travel isn't always pretty. It isn't always comfortable.
Sometimes it hurts; it even breaks your heart.
But that's okay.
The journey changes you; it should change you.
It leaves marks on your memory, on your consciousness,
on your heart, and on your body.
You take something with you.
Hopefully, you leave something good behind.

ANTHONY BOURDAIN

As a volunteer counselor in a teen ministry, I went on all kinds of different camping trips. From camping in the wilderness to camping on a sailboat, from the mountains to the beach…and occasionally a slightly more luxurious place. But the one thing these camp trips seemed to have in common was we usually had one or two unhappy campers. I chalk it up to adolescence and life—you just try to make the best of it, and if you can help them work through a problem, so much the better.

One destination I always looked forward to was a resort in British Columbia. It's the sort of place where anyone, no matter how glum, will eventually have a good time. A place where friendships are forged, hearts are changed, and outlooks improve. At least that's my hope as I spend time with the teen girls in my cabin.

However, a couple of the girls seem destined to make everyone else miserable. They complain about everything. Nothing is good enough for them. The boat trip up here was too rocky, the food is all wrong, the accommodations are uncomfortable. Even the boys aren't quite right. Probably because they're ignoring these two whiny girls. I'd like to ignore them too. Especially when I catch them sneaking cigarettes.

Still, I try to remain positive. I pray for them and try to point them in the right direction, hoping that the speaker's messages will eventually hit pay dirt in these girls' seemingly hardened hearts. I try to get better acquainted with them, try to get them to open up, and try to find some way to connect. But nothing works. Toward the end of camp, I wonder if it's worth it, and I spend more time focusing on the other girls instead. The two complainers seem determined to have a bad camp experience.

They don't seem to care that a pod of beautiful orcas are passing by the inlet. They have no interest in learning to water-ski. They don't want to go canoeing or swimming. I learn that they are here only because some well-meaning person paid their way. They're just counting the hours until we can go home—on that "crummy boat."

On the last night of camp, we hear the news that a classmate back home has been accidentally shot in cross fire by a policeman pursuing a criminal. The boy is dead. And he's a good friend of my two disgruntled camper girls. As sad as it is to hear this heartbreaking news, it is the key to opening them up.

Both the girls are devastated by their friend's death. Suddenly they are falling apart, sobbing, and slightly hysterical. That's when the other camper girls in my cabin totally step up: hugging and talking and praying. We stay up late into the night consoling each other. By the time we go to bed, the climate in that cabin is totally changed. All the girls are close friends. And it's the same the next day.

The boat trip home is amazing. The sadness is still there, but the bonding of friendships and opening of hearts continue. Good has come out of bad, but it never would have happened if we hadn't all been sharing that little cabin together.

Man cannot discover new oceans
unless he has the courage to lose sight of the shore.
ANDRE GIDE

TIP FOR THE DAY

A small, easy-to-pack first aid kit can be created from a small prescription bottle or Altoids tin. Fill with bandages, tweezers, antibiotic cream, antihistamine, pain relievers, etc.

Entry 18
UNDER THE OVERPASS

Leave the road, take the trails.

PYTHAGORAS

Sometimes plans change. You think you'll be on the road for two weeks and suddenly get the urge to go home a few days earlier. Or you stretch your camping trip out longer. Depending on the time of year, this can result in a lack of campground accommodations. Or you can find yourself in the middle of nowhere and too tired to go on.

That is where we are as the day is winding down. We decided to go home a day early, thinking we could make it in one day. But now we're weary. We've traveled for too long, and home is still three hours away. And the closest campground, the one where we should have stopped, is two hours behind us. And it's dinnertime. We are in the middle of nowhere. Unless you've visited eastern Oregon, you might not fully appreciate *nowhere*, but this is it.

Of course, you can't just pull over to the shoulder of a two-lane highway, but we're hoping for some place to stop. We want to eat dinner, get our bearings, and decide if we want to drive the rest of the way home in the dark. I spy an overpass ahead, which is strange, considering there is no crossroad marked on the map. But I point it out, suggesting that at the very least it will be a good place to stop and eat. Chris exits the highway and goes down the gravel road, which basically leads nowhere, and parks under the overpass.

Curious about what this place is, we get out and see that there's a bridge crossing the river, but it's closed to vehicles. Plus, it's unclear where the bridge leads—as we are, remember, in the middle of nowhere. It makes no sense. As we put together some dinner, we joke about being in the Twilight Zone.

But sitting outside to eat, we watch a gorgeous sunset and realize that we've landed in a very delightful spot. Isolated perhaps, but peaceful and pretty and quiet. And, after Chris looks around for a while, he realizes that our trailer and truck are not visible from the road above us. "Why don't we just spend the night?" he suggests. Although I have some concerns—like what if some crazy person decides to pay us a midnight visit—I don't enjoy night-driving either. So I agree.

We continue to sit outside, enjoying the surroundings and dusky sky. Then, thanks to the pitch-black darkness and absolutely no civilization, the stars look brighter than ever above us. Once in a great while a car will pass by, but since this is one of the least-traveled highways in the country, it's mostly just very, very quiet.

Later, we go inside the trailer, deploy the slide-outs, and make ourselves comfortably at home. We use candles and lanterns and the batteries for light. It feels extra cozy. I honestly can't recall a time of more complete isolation. But by the time we go to bed, my imagination is taking off. I've heard stories about what can happen in isolated places like this. What if some criminal decides to come down here and discovers us? My writer's mind starts going down some Stephen King trails, and my heart begins to race. What would we do? Even if our cell phone worked—and it doesn't—it would take a long time to get emergency help in a place like this.

Meanwhile, I can hear Chris sleeping peacefully. So I do what I always do when I'm worried about something: I pray. Soon I'm sleeping peacefully too. And when we get up the next morning, our unexpected camp spot is as quiet and peaceful and beautiful as it was yesterday. I make coffee and fix us breakfast on the gas stove. We linger, sitting outside and enjoying the lovely solitude of this amazingly peaceful site. We are almost reluctant to leave it and go home, but we tell ourselves that perhaps we'll pass this way again…if only we can remember where it is.

The farther one gets into the wilderness,
the greater is the attraction of its lonely freedom.

THEODORE ROOSEVELT

TIP FOR THE DAY

Can't run your RV's coffeemaker? Or you're tent camping but still want to enjoy some coffee? Create a "coffee bag" by filling a coffee filter with ground coffee. Tie it with thread or dental floss, set it in a mug, pour hot water over it and dunk like a tea bag. Wait a few minutes and presto: You have fresh, hot coffee.

Entry 19
THE DEER WHO
CAME TO DINNER

> The continued existence of wildlife and wilderness
> is important to the quality of life of humans.
>
> JIM FOWLER

Camping, to us, is as much about the critters as the geography. As my husband likes to point out, if we put all our animal stories together, we could make a whole book. But that's a different book. Still, I think camping and animals go together. Sometimes quite wonderfully; sometimes not so much.

We're camping with friends in the Wallowa Mountains, aka the "Oregon Alps." It's autumn, and the foliage is already turning red and gold. The air is crisp, sweatshirts and flannel are pulled out, and the campfire is crowded. It's a good time to make a big pot of stew.

It's also the time of year for deer to show up. Probably because it's the cusp of hunting season and deer seem to have an innate sense about this. Bucks with huge racks have come down from the higher elevations—making themselves at home in the campground. It's not unusual to step out of your trailer to discover one or two majestic bucks nestled nearby. We learn to make our exit quietly so we don't startle the strikingly beautiful animals. I know to keep a safe distance, but I can't help but admire them—and get some pics.

We're camping with some friends who have camped here before, and soon they're telling scary buck stories. Or perhaps they're just cautionary tales. But they are rather unsettling. Particularly one unfortunate incident involving a buck at this very campground a year or so ago. A camper, trying to be humorous, fed a deer in a very foolish way. Although the buck didn't intentionally attack this woman, his big sharp antlers inadvertently injured her. She didn't survive. Neither did the buck after the accident was reported. Just one more reason we see signs posted all around, warning us to avoid feeding the wildlife or leaving food unattended outside.

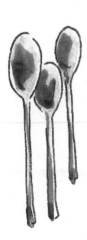

Shortly after I hear this chilling story about the buck and the woman, I notice that some nearby campers are cooking stew... outside. It smells delicious, but it's been left unattended. Then I observe a large buck mosey over to check it out. Using his antlers, he easily tips the lid off the pot and then appears to help himself to the aromatic stew. Apparently it's not hot enough to deter him. I'm watching with wide-eyed fascination, unsure what to do, when a woman leaps out of the trailer, yelling.

Furious at the interloper, she grabs the pot lid and a wooden spoon and starts banging it to scare off the buck. *Right*. This huge buck, not the least bit intimidated by her, continues to help himself to lunch, knocking the pot to the ground. This makes the woman yell louder and, banging her lid, she moves even closer.

"Be careful!" I yell at her. "Bucks can be very dangerous!"

She ignores me, still going after this buck like she thinks she can scare him off and salvage her stew. He lowers his head at her in a threatening way. I yell even louder, telling her to back off. Thankfully she does. But she looks mad as she goes back inside her trailer. And the buck eats the stew.

When the buck finally departs and the woman comes outside again, I tell her about the story I just heard and how dangerous a buck can be. She still seems a little skeptical—not to mention miffed about losing her good stew. But when a camp host shows up to investigate this, he reinforces how serious her situation really was. He sternly reminds her about leaving food unattended.

Sure, I love a good autumn stew as much as anyone, but I wouldn't fight a big buck over it.

If we kill off the wild,
We are killing a part of our souls.
JANE GOODALL

TIP FOR THE DAY

Respect the wildlife in the area you're sharing with them. Don't leave any food or dirty dishes (even pet-food dishes) outside or unattended. Keep camp garbage disposed of or bundled up and out of reach. Even a scented candle can tempt a hungry bear.

MOUNTAIN CLIMBERS

Because in the end, you won't remember the time
you spend working in the office or mowing your lawn.
Climb [that] mountain.

JACK KEROUAC

Although I'd climbed some fairly tall hills, I'd never climbed a real mountain before. Still, I didn't see any reason not to try. I was still young and naïve, and I believed all things were possible. A 10,000-foot mountain? How hard could it be?

Because I'm going with friends who have never climbed this mountain (and only one of them has any climbing experience), I'm in good company, right?

Our plan is to backpack in, camp overnight at the summit, and reach the peak the following day. Then we'll camp overnight again and pack out on the third day. Simple enough.

We hike in, and I quickly realize that carrying a heavy backpack uphill in higher altitudes is hard work—but doable. We make camp and fix dinner from our freeze-dried packets and Sterno stove. We have an enjoyable evening of visiting and stargazing and, because we have a big day tomorrow, we turn in early. But I cannot sleep. Maybe it's because I feel claustrophobic, and the two girls sharing the tiny tent with me seem to be hogging the space. Or maybe I'm just antsy about tomorrow's climb, but it seems to take forever to fall asleep—and even after I do, I wake up again and again.

The next day I'm not feeling terribly energetic, but after breakfast I'm determined to keep up as we begin climbing the mountain. To my relief, despite my mostly sleepless night, my energy is back. But I soon discover we each have a different pace. One pair of friends wants to race ahead. The other pair lags behind. I am in the middle, hiking by myself. Parts of the ascent seem precarious, and I'm stopped and informed by some savvy climbers who are descending that my friends and I don't have the proper equipment. But thanks to the naivete of youth, we all press on.

I'm the third in our group to reach the mountaintop, but eventually we're all up there. We celebrate our victory with granola bars and water, then sign a little book that's kept in a metal box. Then we sit down to soak in the spectacular view…and to rest.

The descent is more tiring than I expect. Once again, I'm hiking alone. When we finally reach our base camp, we're all exhausted. We prepare food and chat, but everyone turns in early. Once again, I feel claustrophobic in our tiny tent. When the other girls fall asleep I'm still wide awake, feeling alone again. Despite being exhausted with aching muscles, I can't sleep. It doesn't help that one girl snores.

So I decide to sleep outside. It's a beautiful summer night and because of the late hour and darkness, the stars are more brilliant than ever. Stunningly brilliant. As I lie out there by myself, I'm tempted to wake everyone and insist they look at the gorgeous stars. But I don't think my friends would appreciate it.

I must admit that I'm feeling rather alone.

I just lie there, staring at the most amazing sky I've ever seen. Suddenly, I'm marveling at the magnitude of God, the Creator of the universe. And I realize that I'm not alone. God is here too. And then I fall asleep.

When I wake with the morning sun, I feel surprisingly refreshed, but then I'm shocked to realize the other tents aren't next to me. I wonder if my friends have abandoned me. I wriggle out of my down mummy-bag and leap to my feet, looking all around to discover the tents are still there—but they are up on the knoll above me. It seems that the others are all still sleeping. I realize I must've slid down the grassy slope during my night of sleeping alone under the stars. But then I'm reminded that I wasn't truly alone. God was right there with me. He always is.

A great many people, and more all the time,
live their entire lives without ever once
sleeping out under the stars.
ALAN S. KESSELHEIM

TIP FOR THE DAY

A hiking headlamp (with the band that goes around your head) can also be strapped around a translucent plastic water jug to provide a good makeshift lantern.

MOVING ON UP

Remember that happiness is a way
of travel—not a destination.

ROY M. GOODMAN

As comfortable as our "long, long" trailer is on the inside, it comes with some challenges. And these little problems are exacerbated by my husband's bad back. He has a ruptured disc, and surgery is probably in his future. After a while, we discover that normal trailer chores—like hitching up, putting the stabilizing jacks up and down, and a few other forms of manual labor—begin to really aggravate Chris's back.

To make matters worse, the large diesel truck is high enough that our hefty Labrador retriever, who's getting older, is unable to jump into the pickup bed. When we take Bailey camping with us, Chris is forced to lift the hefty dog in and out of the pickup. I suggest a doggy ramp, but that turns out to be more trouble than it's worth.

Chris—probably trying to be my macho man—plays down his discomforts. But while we're camping I suspect that his grimaces and slowed gait indicate that he is paying a high price for our oversized and somewhat cumbersome trailer. And when he starts to drag his heels when I suggest a new excursion, I know we have a problem. As much as Chris loves his big diesel pickup and the roomy Arctic Fox trailer, I start to dislike both of them. I don't like seeing my husband in such pain, and I know he's not ready to go under the knife yet. Somehow we need to come up with a better plan.

We agree that we both still love the great outdoors, camping trips, and getting away. But why must it be so difficult? That's when I come up with an idea: What if we exchange our oversized trailer and diesel pickup for a slightly used midsized motor home? I can tell Chris is reluctant to give up his big, manly pickup, but I point out that it won't be much use if he's laid up with a bad back. Not only that, but the truck has a loud engine, and a couple of neighbor ladies have complained about the noise when he warms it up on a cold morning.

I explain that Bailey would be able to enter the RV unassisted. No more lifting a hundred pounds of chocolate Lab! I also point out that if Chris is having back discomfort while traveling, we could easily pull over and he could lie down while I take over the driving. I remind him that my aunt does most of the driving of their motor home. Why couldn't I do that too?

To my surprise, Chris sees my logic. Soon we are shopping for a new camping rig. This time, we know what we do and don't want. We have our list: not brand new, both to save money and because that new-rig smell bothers us. We want an RV that's not too big, not too small—with no slide-outs. It must have high ceilings and a powerful engine. We're not into flashy. We don't want fake-wood cabinets, and we want something that feels well made.

After a few weeks of unsuccessful shopping, we get a call from an RV sales-man. "I found your RV," he tells us. "A Bounder with only one owner. And it was kept in dry storage and barely used." So we go check it out. We sit in the living area, test the solid oak cabinets, check elbow room in the shower, and even try out the bedroom space. Satisfied that it could work for us, we decide to test-drive it.

The engine is great, the mileage is low, and we both agree that this midsized RV is right for us. We drive it home and, a few days later, I'm out there with fabric and sewing machine. I transform the interior from "granny floral" to something that feels campier and comfier. And then we are ready to roll.

For the past 18 years, that Bounder has served us well. We've upgraded almost everything on it: cab chairs, fridge, the bed, and even the toilet. We think it's great, but its years are probably showing. Still, every time we consider making a change—so many tempting trailers and RVs to choose from these days—we always come home to our Bounder and decide it's just what we need.

It's comfortable, kind of like an old slipper. Every time I'm inside of it, especially if it's been a while, I feel warmly welcomed. It seems that our Bounder (just like Chris and me) still has many miles to go. And we are all looking forward to what's ahead.

Sooner or later we must realize there is no station,
No one place to arrive at once and for all.
The true joy of life is the trip.

ROBERT J. HASTINGS

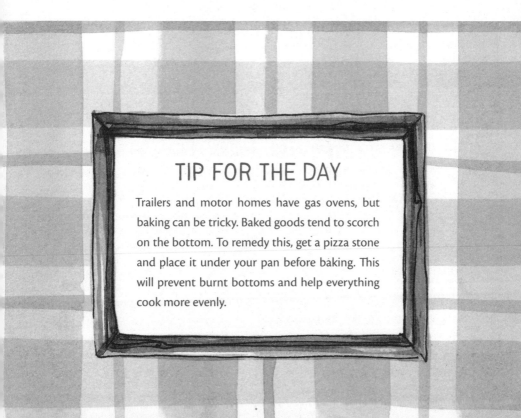

TIP FOR THE DAY

Trailers and motor homes have gas ovens, but baking can be tricky. Baked goods tend to scorch on the bottom. To remedy this, get a pizza stone and place it under your pan before baking. This will prevent burnt bottoms and help everything cook more evenly.

Entry 22
ROAD OF NO RETURN

Wanderlust: *n.* a strong desire for or impulse to
wander or travel and explore the world.

WIKTIONARY

Toward the end of a long motor home trip, we decide to try an out-of-the-way campground on our way home. Just for one night. We know nothing about this place, and, because we're off the beaten path, our cell phones have no connectivity to do some quick research. But, hey—the place is in the book and on the map. Why not check it out? How bad could it be?

And if we don't like the look or feel of the campground, we'll look for another spot. Perhaps a state park or roadside pullout. As we get closer to where it's supposed to be, we notice heavy clouds gathering above us. We hope we'll get to the campground before this thunderstorm cuts loose. I'm being the navigator, reading the map and estimating how far we have to go. We slow down as we come to a town with a population of about 37. But maybe there is someone around who can give us information or directions. We drive through the "business loop," and all seems rather dark and dodgy. Or maybe it's just the effect of the black clouds overhead. It's about to rain, so we can't waste time chatting with the locals. *Let's just get to the campground and get settled*, we decide.

At the end of the business loop, we notice a small group of people outside a tiny restaurant/store. They stare at us with great interest, and we can't imagine what's so compelling about our rather modest motor home or the Jeep Wrangler we tow behind us. But unless it's our imagination, they seem slightly amused. It's almost as if they're chuckling as we turn down the graveled road that, according to the sign, is supposed to lead to the campground. But on we go.

On this road, which soon turns into a narrow dirt path with lots of huge ruts and protruding rocks, we realize this is not going to work. Not only is the road a breakdown waiting to happen, it will turn into a mucky, muddy mess once the rain hits. And there is no sign of any campground ahead. For all we know, it could be miles away. In fact, we wonder if the campground exists anymore. We don't intend to find out. But now what? Giant raindrops are splattering our windshield.

"We can't turn around," Chris says with a worried look. When I ask why, he points out the deep ditches along both sides of the road. Given those ditches and all the loose dirt, we'd surely get stuck.

"We're going to have to back up," he says.

"Back up?" I gasp, trying to imagine how that's even possible.

"First we have to unhitch the Jeep," he explains.

"You probably should back it up too—until you reach the main road. Then wait for me in that town." Realizing we're in a rather dire situation, I quickly agree. In the pouring rain and uneven surface, we work to maneuver the hitch, finally managing to disengage the Jeep. The dirt road is already getting muddy as I start backing up. It feels weird to drive backward, but I don't want to risk getting the Jeep stuck in those ditches and blocking the Bounder.

It takes about an hour to get back to the tiny town, where I'm sure those people are now safely indoors, laughing their heads off at the "crazy campers." I'm guessing they knew all about that nasty bit of road and that it was a disaster waiting to happen. Too bad we didn't think to stop and ask first. As we re-hitch the Jeep to the RV, we get soaked to the skin, but we're so thankful not to be stuck on that muddy road that we don't even care.

And the next time we see bystanders laughing at us, we'll probably stop to find out why. Before it's too late.

If you think adventures are dangerous,
try routine. It's lethal.
PAULO COELHO

TIP FOR THE DAY

Recycle an empty laundry detergent container (the big plastic kind with a spout on the bottom) into a hand-washing station. Duct tape on a small plastic cup to serve as a soap holder, loop a hand towel through the container's handle, fill with water, and place outside on a picnic table.

HER LAST CAMPING TRIP

You get guys around a campfire, and they start telling their stories. That's the fellowship that they want to be in.

JOHN ELDREDGE

My aunt, like my grandma, was a good outdoorswoman. Whether it was hunting or fishing or camping with her husband, Bob, she was always game. Auntie Carol, as my sister and I lovingly called her, helped to raise us and, I like to think, helped inspire us to partake in outdoorsy-campy things. Even her kitchen dishware set had a fun, "campy" look to it.

I remember one autumn when my aunt and uncle were getting ready to go hunting. They posed in front of their pickup, wearing only their new sets of matching long johns. I know there's a photo of that somewhere, but their happily grinning faces are still indelible in my mind.

My aunt went through some rough years—before and after losing her beloved husband. Sometimes she'd go "missing." Her car would be in her driveway, but she couldn't be found. We all eventually discovered that she would be outside, sitting at the dining table of their old camper—probably reminiscing over happier times. I remember sitting out there with her once, and I *got it*. The small space felt peaceful and contained and secure. I wasn't surprised she liked it. I sometimes do that very same thing in my motor home when it's parked right outside our house. I can't really explain why I like it, but I do.

Several years after my aunt lost her husband, she began to suffer from early-onset Alzheimer's. At first we just thought it was forgetfulness and aging, but the disease progressed steadily. Although my cousin and mom were trying to help her, we all knew it wouldn't be long until she would require residential care. Naturally, we were all sad about this. She was such a sweet, jovial soul, and it was hard to see her frustrated and confused, simply not her old self.

During this era, it occurred to me that we should take Auntie Carol camping. I told my sister, and we both agreed that our aunt should have one last camping trip before she went into a full-time care facility. Maybe she wouldn't even remember it later, but at least she would enjoy it at the time. And we wanted to enjoy one last happy time with her.

The plan was for me to park our trailer at our favorite beachside campground. My sister and I would stay there, and my mother and cousin and aunt would stay in a cabin next door. My sister and I would provide the "camp experience," and my mother and cousin would take care of my aunt.

I can't say that it all went perfectly smoothly (my mom and cousin can attest to that), but I can say that with the ocean right there in front of us, combined with good camp food and some hearty laughs, Auntie Carol seemed to come around. Because she grew up in an Oregon coastal town, the experience stirred something in her memory bank, and she shared many of her favorite old stories with us. All in all, it was a delightful camping trip, but the best times by far were spent around the campfire, laughing, talking, singing goofy songs. For a few sparkling moments, Auntie Carol was her old self again. And we were all happy campers.

I see my path, but I don't know where it leads.
Not knowing where I'm going is what inspires me to travel it.
ROSALIA DE CASTRO

TIP FOR THE DAY

Even the most basic camping trip requires a few essentials.
Here's a minimalist starter list:

- cooler that closes securely
- hand sanitizer and soap
- matches/lighter and fire-starting materials
- pail and shovel
- rope/cords
- water for drinking/cooking/cleaning

PLUMBING IN THE VINEYARD

Our lessons come from the journey,
not the destination.

DON WILLIAMS JR.

When our young granddaughter moves to a neighboring state (and she can't visit every weekend anymore), we promise to visit during the first week of summer break. She asks us to bring the RV and get a campground with a nice big pool. So I do my research and reserve a spot at a nice campground a half hour from our granddaughter's home. It happens to be at a vineyard, which appears to be a very attractive place.

It's about a three-hour drive, but with pretty scenery and nice June weather, it's enjoyable. Chris and I arrive at the campground with plenty of time to get our campsite arranged. The place looks nice, and since we don't pick up our granddaughter until tomorrow, we hope to check it out after we're set up.

We haven't camped yet this season, so we know there's the usual "first of the season" chores to do. Also, since we haven't been out since last summer, there's the usual attempts to remember how to set everything up. It's surprising how easy it is to forget how to lower jacks, put out the awning, and do other ordinary chores.

We start with disconnecting our tow Jeep and parking it out of the way. Then, as Chris puts down the electric stabilizing jacks and connects the electricity and water, I do some general cleaning. As I'm wiping down the kitchen countertops, I notice there's water shooting out from beneath the kitchen sink.

I yell at Chris to turn off the water, and I start cleaning up the mess. He comes inside to investigate—only to discover the pipes, which are brittle plastic, have broken. And since it's impossible to just shut down one section of pipes, like you can do in a house, there is no plumbing anywhere in the RV. Not exactly fun.

"Maybe I can fix it," my handy husband says optimistically.

"You mean while we're here camping?" I ask.

"Why not?" He reminds me that he recently helped the plumber to re-plumb our little beach cabin and it wasn't that hard. Plus, there are some great new products available that he thinks will work for an RV. I still question how that'll be any fun for him, but he points out that the granddaughter and I will probably find fun "girl things" to do—things he's not interested in anyway. So he can play plumber. I agree with his plan.

Our first stop is the hardware store, which isn't too far away. We buy plumbing parts and some water containers to get us by while the pipes are being fixed. It's not convenient to use a jug of water to flush the toilet, but when I consider the pioneers, I realize we're not truly roughing it.

I quickly introduce our granddaughter to our rustic conditions, but she's not concerned. She's just glad we have a nearby pool to play in. And I'm glad there's a big shower room and bathroom so conveniently located.

For the next week, Chris plays plumber (occasionally taking a break to be with us girls). Meanwhile, our granddaughter and I hang out at the pool and other kid places that ten-year-olds enjoy, because Chris gets more accomplished when we're not underfoot. But I must admit there are times when I wish I could play plumber and he could play with his energetic grandchild. As far as the two adults enjoying the vineyard? Not so much.

When the week ends, I'm not sure which of us is more tired. But at least the plumbing is nearly fixed and our granddaughter got plenty of time with her nana. And from now on, we'll make sure we're fully functional before taking off for the first trip of the season.

Do the difficult things while they are easy
and do the great things while they are small.
A journey of a thousand miles
must begin with a single step.

LAO TZU

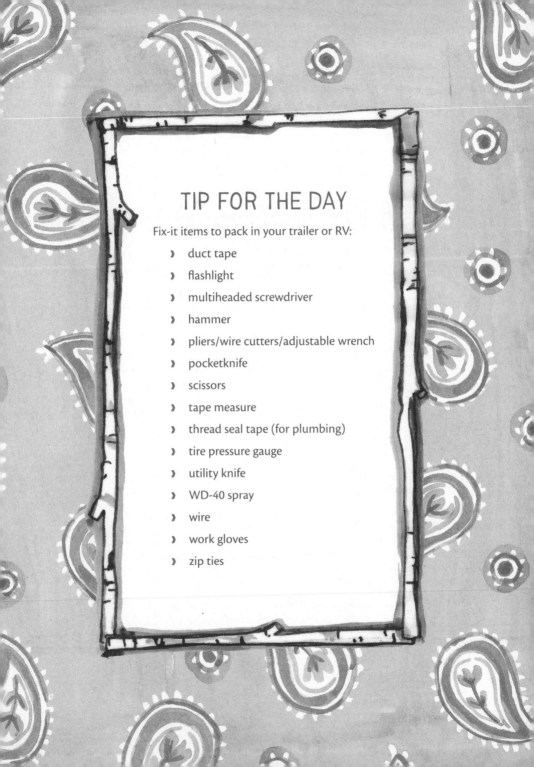

TIP FOR THE DAY

Fix-it items to pack in your trailer or RV:

- ❭ duct tape
- ❭ flashlight
- ❭ multiheaded screwdriver
- ❭ hammer
- ❭ pliers/wire cutters/adjustable wrench
- ❭ pocketknife
- ❭ scissors
- ❭ tape measure
- ❭ thread seal tape (for plumbing)
- ❭ tire pressure gauge
- ❭ utility knife
- ❭ WD-40 spray
- ❭ wire
- ❭ work gloves
- ❭ zip ties

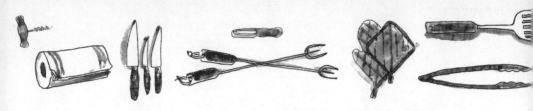

RATTLESNAKE FOR LUNCH, ANYONE?

I always encourage people to get out there,
travel the world, see new things, experience new people,
experience new food, experience new culture…
That helps you to grow and be your best self.

KARAMO BROWN

In more civilized and populated parts of the country, my home state (Oregon) is considered to be fairly remote, and, if folks are being honest, perhaps a bit back-woodsish. When visiting a sophisticated, cosmopolitan city, I'll often admit that I live in the sticks. But it's not a complaint. I'm grateful to live in a less-populated state with lots of natural beauty to be enjoyed. Camping opportunities here are almost unlimited. We have mountains and deserts and beaches…oh, my!

So if you're camping in Oregon and really want to follow the *unbeaten road*, go to Imnaha. It's in the northeastern-most corner of the state, and one of the most remote towns in the country. Although Imnaha has a post office and a school, it's unincorporated. The population is around 150. I think the real reason this settlement remains so isolated is that the highway pretty much ends there. On the other side of Imnaha you'll discover the Snake River Gorge—with no bridge to get you across to a somewhat less-remote region in Idaho. Suffice it to say, Imnaha isn't a metropolis.

But the place really comes to life when they celebrate Imnaha Canyon Day in the fall. Besides a parade, a rodeo, and a few other festivities, the town hosts their renowned Bear and Rattlesnake Feed. Eager partakers line up to enjoy this culinary luncheon treat. I know because I waited in that line once. Let me state clearly: It wasn't my idea. As a child, I was a finicky eater and, as an adult, I've never been into gourmet cuisine like calamari or escargot. And certainly not rattlesnake!

But we are camping with friends and family, and because they're all champing at the bit to attend the "Feed," I agree. If nothing else, it should be interesting…as a spectator. After all, I lived in a third-world country where people ate all kinds of disgusting foods like beetles, wild boar, and crocodile. And it might be entertaining to watch my husband and some of the others gagging over rattlesnake. I don't admit it to anyone, but I don't plan to eat a single bite.

Chris and some of the guys claim they're hungry as they join the growing line of those waiting to be served this delectable treat. I'm in no hurry. I act like I want to see "more of the town." This is a joke; there really isn't any *more* of this town. But a couple of the women who've been camping with us decide to do the same. I'm guessing they're about as eager as I am to eat snake. So we stroll around and check things out. By the time we mosey back to the lunch line, it's stretched down the street and *snaking* around the corner.

The women and I continue to visit as the line inches forward. We joke about the idea of eating rattlesnake, but the other women seem willing to give the exotic menu item a try. I'm not interested. I think I can handle the bear meat okay, but the idea of biting into rattlesnake? Well, as much as I'd like to be that adventurous, the idea does not sit well with me.

So we're finally inside the building, and I'm next in line when I hear someone cry out: "Oh, no! We're out of rattlesnake!" There are lots of moans and groans, but then a fellow says there's more in the freezer, asking a gal to go start defrosting it. I'm imagining her picking up a frozen-stiff coiled rattler and tossing it into the microwave. Not so appetizing.

"You can wait for it," an apron-clad woman tells me, "or save your ticket and come back later."

"That's okay," I tell her. "I'll just have the bear stew." Relieved, I carry my lunch outside and join the guys, who act like they're still picking snake bones out of their teeth. According to them, "Rattler tastes just like chicken," but I'm happy to take their word for it.

Because the bear stew is quite good!

We keep moving forward, opening new doors,
doing new things, because we're curious.
And curiosity keeps leading us down new paths.

WALT DISNEY

TIP FOR THE DAY

If your campsite has electric hookups, consider packing a slow cooker in your RV or trailer. Put in a roast (or rattlesnake), along with onions and veggies in the morning. After a day of outdoor explorations, come home to a delicious homemade dinner.

BEST BIRTHDAY PARTY

I see retirement as just another of these reinventions,
another chance to do new things
and be a new version of myself.

WALT MOSSBERG

There's no better time on the Oregon coast than autumn. For one thing, the summertime tourists have mostly evacuated. The towns are still lively but not overly busy. And the best part—especially for campers—is that the weather is usually sunny and mild.

For that reason, we decide to meet up with my sister for a weekend of coastal camping. And we bring our mom too. Our destination is a state park not far from the beach. My sister brings her camp trailer and two kids. In late afternoon, we park our rigs side by side in a woodsy campground next to the sand dunes. Before long, we're settled in, sharing food around a crackling campfire. We're ready to relax and let the good times roll. The kids are energetic, but the grownups are a little worn out. The anticipation of a relaxing weekend is appealing.

As we're visiting around the fire, it occurs to someone (probably Mom) that tomorrow is Chris's dad's birthday. Frank is recently retired and has relocated to the coast. In fact, he and his wife, Pat, don't live too far away from where we're camping. So my mother, a woman who loves to celebrate almost anything, suggests we invite them to our camp for a birthday dinner party tomorrow.

That's a nice idea, but I have two reservations—and they're not at the Ritz Carlton. My first concern is minor: We'd all hoped to enjoy a relaxing, stress-free weekend. But Frank is a dear and it would be worth the effort to make him feel special. My other concern is that Chris's mom can be unpredictable at family get-togethers. I've been married to Chris long enough to know how many ways a gathering can go sideways when Pat is involved. Particularly for her husband.

Still, I keep my worries to myself. For all I know, Chris's parents will be busy tomorrow. But before Chris checks in with his parents the next morning, I suggest he pretend it's not for Frank's birthday. Just invite them to join us for dinner—and it can be a surprise party. That might make this go more smoothly. And maybe his parents already have plans for the evening. Okay, I'm hoping they do.

But when Chris checks in with his parents, dinner is a go. Chris even invites a couple of his dad's friends who live nearby to join us. So, putting the kibosh on relaxing all day, we get busy. We make trips to town, gathering birthday gifts, food and drinks, cake and ice cream, and lots of birthday decorations (from the dollar store). Even my sister's kids help. We put out balloons and crepe paper, tablecloths, fresh flowers, candles—the works. Our combined campsites look so festive that passersby pause to admire the scene.

I'm a little nervous as the dinner hour approaches. I don't express my worries to the others, although I know Chris is having similar thoughts. We both know that anything could happen tonight. Frank's friends show up first and seem delighted with the campy birthday party idea. Then we see Frank's van pull up, and Chris and I go out to meet them. But Frank is alone. He politely apologizes: "Pat has a headache and can't make it. I hope you don't mind it's just me."

We try not to act too elated as we lead Frank over to our campsite, where everyone shouts, "Surprise! Happy Birthday!" The delighted look on Frank's face is priceless…and worth every bit of effort. We all have a beautiful evening. Afterward, Frank gratefully thanks us, saying it is one of his best birthday celebrations ever.

I collect memories. I look for opportunities to try new things, go to new places, and meet new people all the time.

MARCEL WANDERS

TIP FOR THE DAY

Keep a small box of party supplies (the dollar store is a great resource) on hand for unexpected celebrations out on the trail.

Entry 27

LOLLY THE BEAR

Some people talk to animals.
Not many listen though.
That's the problem.

A.A. MILNE

As we all know, there are many ways to camp. Sometimes you rough it; sometimes you camp in style. That's how it feels in our beach cabin—comfort and style. Don't get me wrong; it wasn't always like that. We spent a few years rehabbing what some would call a "tear-down." During that time, we camped in our RV, which we kept parked in the backyard. So even when our cabin starts to resemble a five-star hotel suite, we still think of it as campy.

That's greatly due to the setting. Nestled in coastal pines, within walking distance from the beach and not far from an RV park, our lot feels like a campground. We even have a fire pit we enjoy on a cool foggy afternoon or evening.

But because of our location, we also seem to get more than our fair share of critters. Besides birds, squirrels, and raccoons, we get the occasional beaver and otter too. But it's the bears that really get our attention. We've seen more bears at our beach cabin than anywhere else.

There's the bear who empties the birdfeeder (I learn that birdfeeders are a bad idea in bear country). Beyond that, we have bears who steal candles from our deck. (Maybe they need to light their caves?) But the organic slug bait for my flowerpots? Well, I just hope it doesn't make the bears sick. By now we have a bear-proof garbage can. But a lot of the vacation cabins don't. That's when you wake to overturned garbage cans and trash strewn all about.

When the nearby restaurant has their dumpster tipped over, everyone knows that only a huge bear could do that. Our neighborhood is warned to remain on high alert for bears. Apparently, the bears woke up early from hibernation and food is scarce. This means break-ins are becoming common. Some neighbors claim the bears are becoming a nuisance. They want them removed and relocated, but Chris and I like bears. We hope they'll get to stay. Even when a bear breaks into our daughter-in-law's car (she left fast-food remnants inside, with the window open a crack), we still don't want the bears removed.

One night, our granddaughter leaves one of those colorful oversized lollipops outside, wrapped in waxed paper. The next day we find the smoothed-out wrapper with the lollipop stick laid neatly upon it—almost like a thank-you, from a very neat bear. Not long after that, we're awakened by a noise on the deck outside our bedroom. We peek out to see a large bear with its nose pressed to the bedroom window, probably looking for another lollipop. We admit that it's a little unsettling to be separated from a bear by only a pane of glass, but we chuckle and name her Lolly.

One early morning, Chris quietly tells me to come outside. There, we stand motionless in front of our cabin with our dog, Audrey, watching a mama bear and her two adorable cubs less than 50 feet away. Okay, we're not stupid. We know this is potentially dangerous, but we don't make a move, and the mama seems okay. We imagine it's Lolly, here to show us her babies. But when Audrey wags her tail, Lolly sends her cubs up a pair of trees. It's an incredible scene and, as much as we want to linger, we know it's time to slip back into the house. But it feels like Lolly simply wanted to show us her babies.

Clearly, animals know more than we think,
and think a great deal more than we know.

IRENE M. PEPPERBERG

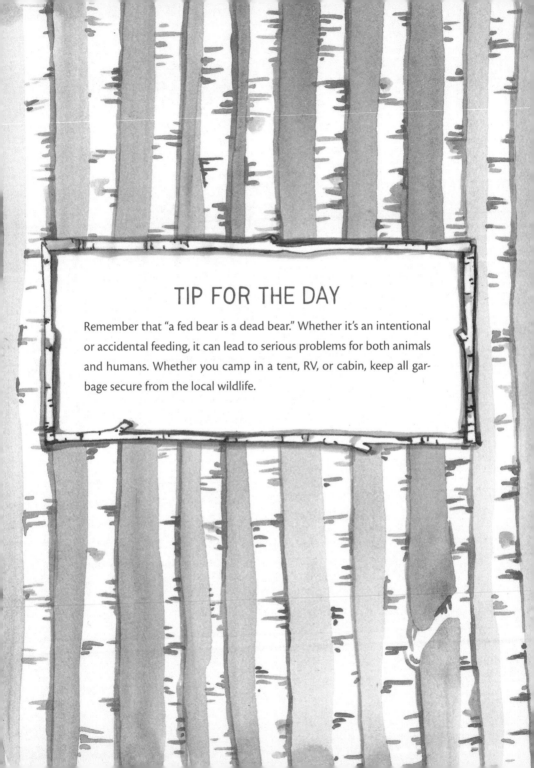

TIP FOR THE DAY

Remember that "a fed bear is a dead bear." Whether it's an intentional or accidental feeding, it can lead to serious problems for both animals and humans. Whether you camp in a tent, RV, or cabin, keep all garbage secure from the local wildlife.

THE GETAWAY

The purpose of life…is to live it,
to taste experience to the utmost,
to reach out eagerly and without fear
for newer and richer experience.

ELEANOR ROOSEVELT

Sometimes you just need a little break. Even if it's just for the weekend. When a friend recommends a hot-springs camping experience, I'm a bit wary. For one thing, "Cindy" is an old hippie. I mean the kind of woman who's done some things…been to some places. Stuff I'm glad to have missed. Besides that, this is Oregon. I've heard some hot-springs tales—and some of those stories made the news. Some hot-springs areas, besides being risqué (as in no swimsuits required) sound downright scary and dangerous. But Cindy assures me this place is not like that.

So, after a long, hard mountain winter (and waiting for a spring that never seems to come), I suggest to Chris that we should give this hot-springs place a try. I make a reservation at the campground and, on Friday afternoon, we drive the motor home over the mountain and down to a region that's a bit more moderate than home.

It's just getting dusky as we arrive at the right milepost. But the entrance sign to the campground is almost invisible. Maybe they don't want anyone to see it? We turn in anyway. But now the road gets narrow, dark, shadowy...almost spooky. It doesn't help that we go for a ways, yet see no any signs of other campers—or cars, or anyone. We slowly proceed, not sure what to think or do. There's no place to turn around, so we continue, reminding ourselves that we don't have to stay here. If the place turns into a scene from a Stephen King movie, we will hightail it out of here and go straight home.

Eventually, we turn a corner and see that there are other campers here. To our relief, although a few of them look like hippie buses, most of them seem normal. And sure enough there is a large lodge building. Suddenly feeling hopeful, we decide that Cindy hasn't steered us wrong after all. I go into the lodge, which looks nice, and get us registered. They give me a map and point me in the right direction. Before long we are parked in our space and setting up our camp. It's reassuring to see that the other trailers and RVs parked around us seem "normal."

On the campground map, we can see where

the hot-spring pools are located, and one appears to be close by. I ask Chris if he wants to try it out, and he gives me a skeptical look. "What if they're not wearing swimsuits?" he asks.

I roll my eyes, acting like this thought hasn't crossed my mind. "Of course, they'll be wearing swimsuits," I assure him. "This place is perfectly fine." We get into our swimsuits (which I always store in the RV), and, with big towels wrapped around us, we venture to the pool area. I am nervous as we go through the gate. We can see a few heads bobbing around in what looks like a normal, albeit surprisingly large, swimming pool. But because of the steam from the water, it's impossible to see if they're wearing suits.

Chris and I exchange glances, then hesitantly enter the hot pool. I'm not sure what we'll do if we discover we're overdressed, but, to our relief, it soon becomes apparent that everyone is wearing swimsuits. We relax, soaking in the marvelous hot water until winter's chill seems to have melted away.

By the next day, we discover that the hot springs are a delight—and the acres of gardens and hiking trails throughout this amazingly well-maintained campground are spectacular. The people are great too. It's no surprise that this magical place becomes one of our favorite weekend getaways.

Traveling carries with it the curse of
being at home everywhere and yet nowhere,
for wherever one is, some part of oneself
remains on another continent.

MARGOT FONTEYN

TIP FOR THE DAY

If you're camping in a moderate climate with water nearby, be prepared for mosquitoes. As an alternative to DEET products, citronella buckets, and long pants and sleeves, consider making sage bundles to use on a campfire. Mosquitoes don't like the sage smoke. And you can "smoke" your outer clothing for even more protection.

STINKING WATER CAMPGROUND

A drop of water, if it could write out its own history,
would explain the universe to us.

LUCY LARCOM

I'd always wanted to visit Jackson Hole. So when a friend invites me to a writers' conference there, I'm all in. Never mind that I don't really enjoy writers' conferences. I find them stressful. Writers striving to make good impressions? It's too much pressure to "perform." Then again, it's Jackson Hole. I want to go.

Of course, when Chris finds out I want to go, he wants to go too. We decide to turn it into a big camping trip. We'll follow the Oregon Trail (backward) and stop at some of the national parks and just have fun. Off we go, enjoying the sights and trailer-camping all the way there.

By the time we reach Jackson Hole, we're a little worn out. We've mostly dry-camped everywhere because of "no full hookups" (no water or electric). As a result, we feel like crusty pioneers. We are looking forward to electricity and running water. I'm eager for a long, hot shower, a good shampoo, and doing some laundry. We have a day and a half to accomplish this before the conference starts. And I sure don't want to attend a writers' conference feeling like a dirty old camper. Plus, we want to enjoy this interesting Old West town.

I made our reservation at the campground two months ago. It's a good thing I did. We quickly learn that not only is this slightly lackluster campground filled to capacity, but all the others within a 60-mile radius are full as well. Besides that, all hotels, bed-and-breakfasts, and all other forms of accommodation are booked too. We hear that Jackson Hole has gone through a recent population explosion, followed by a building boom that's in process. As a result, there's a serious lack of housing. Homeowners outside city limits are renting rooms as well as RV spaces. Jackson Hole has a serious case of No Vacancy. And, although the RV park is sort of bare-bones, we realize we're lucky to have a place to park our trailer. We quickly settle in.

Eager to lose the camp dust, I hit the shower. As the hot water runs over me, I notice something. Something seriously stinks! At first, I think something's wrong with our trailer. Is the intake water hose connected to the wrong source? Because what's coming out of our shower smells almost like sewer water. I quickly dry off and, feeling more unclean than before, I hurry to investigate what's going on.

Our clean, white potable-water hose is connected

to the fresh water spigot that's assigned to our camp spot, and everything seems to be in order. Chris comes over to see what I'm doing and, barely dressed and with dripping hair, I explain the problem.

"Oh, yeah, someone just told me that the water here is kinda smelly," he explains.

"Smelly?" I wrinkle my nose. "It stinks!"

"Yeah. I hear the nickname for this campground is *Stinking Water*."

"Seriously?" Is he pulling my leg? He assures me that's what it is and we'll have to make the best of it. At least until the writers' conference is over and we leave Jackson Hole. Naturally, I'm wondering about laundry and bathing and stinking hair. I can imagine people at the writers' conference plugging their noses around me.

We start brainstorming solutions. Before long, we have something of a plan. We can get drinking water in town, and, we hope, find a Laundromat and wash our clothes there too. As for bathing and hair washing? We'll have to be like pioneers and have a bucket bath. We agree the only thing the stinking water is good for is the toilet.

By the time I'm at the writers' conference, I'm a little weary, and using more perfume than usual. I feel like I've come down the Oregon Trail *backward* and that I've been bathing like my ancestor pioneers did on the wagon train. I hope I don't stink too badly. Fortunately, no one seems to notice—at least they don't mention it—and the writers' conference turns out to be the best one ever!

Some people have such a talent
for making the best of a bad situation
that they go around creating bad situations
so they can make the best of them.

JEAN KERR

TIP FOR THE DAY

Before leaving for your camping
trip, freeze water jugs (or recycled
juice/milk jugs) and use them in
your ice chests—and for drinking
water (if your campground water
isn't potable).

FIREWORKS ON THE FOURTH

Healing can only happen when people are willing to shift.
IYANLA VANZANT

Our granddaughter's birthday falls within the Fourth of July week, so we got into the tradition of taking her to the beach cabin to celebrate. It was always fun to participate in the small town's Fourth festivities—parades, carnival, open market, air shows...and finally the gorgeous fireworks show over the coastal estuary. We all had many happy memories there.

But then came the year we sold the beach cabin—the same year our granddaughter turned into a teenager. Unhappy about the loss of the beach cabin, our grandchild asks if we can take the motor home and camp at the coast during the Fourth. That sounds like fun, so I find a campground in a handy location. The plan is for my granddaughter and me to camp—just the two of us—while Chris, who has commitments at home, will join us on the Fourth.

At the campground, which is right in town, we discover that our campsite looks directly over the river, and it's close to where they launch the fireworks. Perfect! But all my granddaughter seems to care about is whether or not there's Wi-Fi. Okay, fine. We find out that Wi-Fi is available and get the password. However, we quickly discover we can't access it from 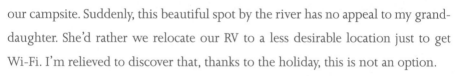 our campsite. Suddenly, this beautiful spot by the river has no appeal to my granddaughter. She'd rather we relocate our RV to a less desirable location just to get Wi-Fi. I'm relieved to discover that, thanks to the holiday, this is not an option.

To find Wi-Fi access, my granddaughter must visit a nearby public-use area and sit in the gazebo. Not ideal, but at least she can connect with her friends. But after a while, I wonder if she ever disconnects from her friends. When I question this "e-addiction," my previously sweet granddaughter reacts like a snarky teenager. Still, we discuss this, and I attempt to establish some general rules. Somehow, I entice her to do a few things in town. However, it becomes crystal clear that she and her phone are attached at the hip.

When I try to get her to engage in Independence Day activities or simply look at the Thunderbird planes roaring across the sky, she barely looks up. I become more and more frustrated. I miss the little girl who used to love these things—why do they grow up so fast?

Still, I try to keep positive. We get crabs for her birthday dinner. We do the few things in town that seem to interest her—not necessarily me. But, hey, it's her birthday. And anything that can disconnect her from that stupid phone is worth it. Despite my attempts to make this fun, she complains a lot. All she seems to want is Wi-Fi connection. And it's wearing me down. I ask myself why she even wanted to come to the beach in the first place. She's not truly here.

On the Fourth, Chris shows up and doesn't understand why I'm so frustrated. My granddaughter and I have always gotten along so well. He doesn't seem to understand the whole teenage thing or Wi-Fi addiction. I try to explain, hoping he'll intervene, because I honestly feel that I can't stand it another minute. It comes to a head that evening when my granddaughter has no interest in the fireworks. She'd rather sit in the gazebo and chat with her friends. That's when I give her another kind of fireworks. I tell her that she's been selfish and that I don't know why we went to the effort to bring her here. She says a few things too. Neither of us really enjoys the spectacular display of fireworks, reflecting over the river and echoing off the hills on the other side.

Fortunately, we both cool off the next day. I get a rather sweet apology and a morsel of gratitude. And then my granddaughter and I go down to the river bank and, while the tide is out, we dig clams. We make clam chowder for dinner, and I think that if I can be patient, she will eventually outgrow this awkward adolescent era. Meanwhile, I'll make sure she knows that I love her... unconditionally.

You don't choose your family.
They are God's gift to you,
as you are to them.

DESMOND TUTU

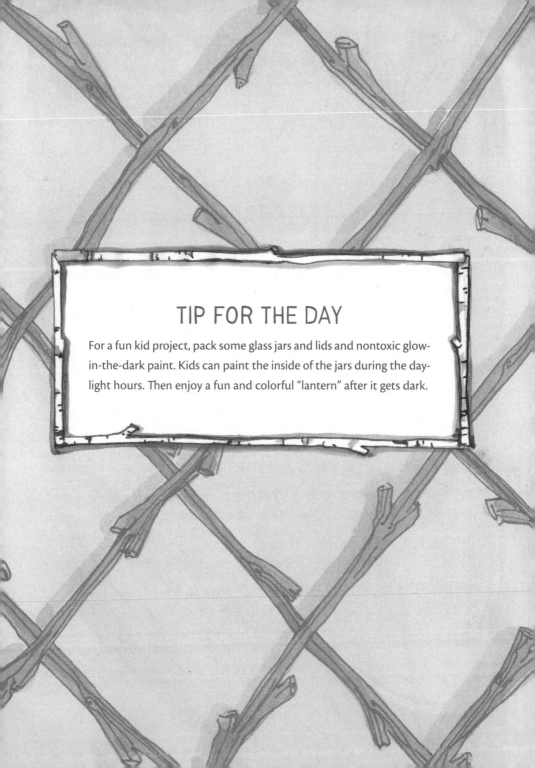

TIP FOR THE DAY

For a fun kid project, pack some glass jars and lids and nontoxic glow-in-the-dark paint. Kids can paint the inside of the jars during the daylight hours. Then enjoy a fun and colorful "lantern" after it gets dark.

Entry 31
RV DOG

The dog lives for the day, the hour, even the moment.

ROBERT FALCON SCOTT

Because we often arrange for a house-sitter to manage our home while we're gone, we don't always take our dogs with us. Sometimes, due to medical issues or concern for long hours on the road, it just seems kinder to leave a pet at home with a good caregiver. But if it's a short trip, where a dog can get some enjoyment, it can be fun to take them along. Of course, this means extra preparations and, because our dogs tend to be rather large Labrador retrievers, we have to accommodate for their space needs too.

The first time we take our yellow Lab, Audrey, with us, our camping trip begins with no problems. We "adopted" Audrey when she was two and, although we don't know if she's been camping before, she's always been a great traveler. You open a vehicle door and she eagerly hops in, even if you're not going anywhere. She loves to go.

We know that Audrey's previous home, where her siblings were little dogs (think Chihuahuas), she experienced some troubles, which is why we gave her a new home. But Audrey has always been a pure delight, and now we are eager to see how she does at camping. Naturally, she is eager to go.

Just as I used to do with our previous Lab, Bailey, I place a dog bed beneath the dining table of our motor home. Audrey, like many dogs, loves sleeping in a sheltered spot. She particularly likes being under a table. I think it gives her a secure feeling. And we don't mind giving up our table, because we usually eat outside when we're camping anyway.

So we take Audrey out to the motor home and barely get the door open before she eagerly bounds inside. She instantly figures out that her place is under the table, where she makes herself at home. Satisfied that she'll be a good traveler, we head off. Audrey seems perfectly content in her special space and doesn't budge during the first leg of our journey. We plan to stop for lunch at one of our favorite restaurants along the way, then continue for a few more hours before we reach camp.

When we make our lunch stop, parking in an RV area, we take Audrey outside to do her thing. Soon, she happily returns to her bed and we give her a doggy treat and go have a nice, leisurely lunch. When we return to our RV, we notice a large motor home parked by our rig. On the dashboard, a pair of Chihuahuas are perched. They yip at us, acting like they rule the world as well as their motor home.

That's when we notice that Audrey—our big

yellow Labrador—is perched on our dashboard too. She looks quite pleased with herself, as if she belongs up there—like she is queen of the RV. And like she thinks she's a dainty little Chihuahua and not an 80-pound Lab.

I can't help but laugh as we go inside. Of course, it makes sense in a twisted way. In her previous home, she was the puppy that was raised by older Chihuahua-type dogs. Sometimes, she must think she's a small dog too. I gently scold her for being on the dashboard instead of her nice bed. Of course, she takes it in stride. But happy to see that we're back, she gladly returns to her spot under the table.

As we drive, I realize that she probably just wanted to look out the window while waiting for us. And, really, our huge dashboard has plenty of room for a dog her size. In fact, it's not a bad place for her. I decide to put a piece of carpeting up there, to protect the dashboard, and we will allow her to occupy that space while we're not around.

So, if you ever see a big yellow Lab—looking slightly oversized as she sits on the dashboard of a parked Bounder motor home—you can bet it's Audrey. The Labrador retriever who thinks she's a Chihuahua.

Dogs are not our whole life,
but they make our lives whole.

ROGER A. CARAS

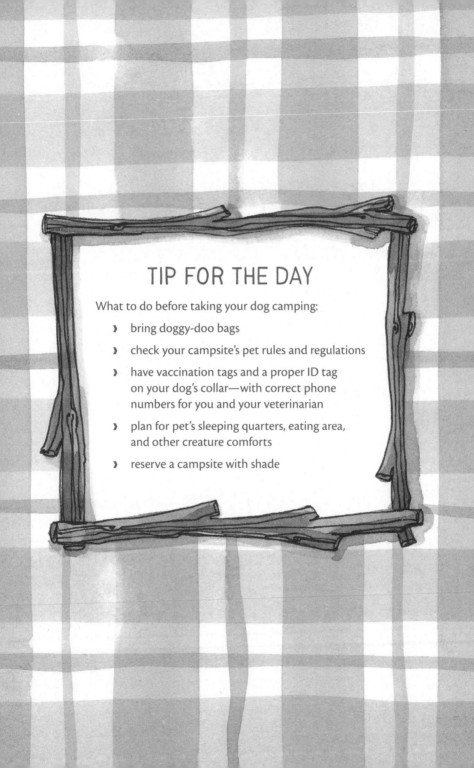

TIP FOR THE DAY

What to do before taking your dog camping:

- ❯ bring doggy-doo bags
- ❯ check your campsite's pet rules and regulations
- ❯ have vaccination tags and a proper ID tag on your dog's collar—with correct phone numbers for you and your veterinarian
- ❯ plan for pet's sleeping quarters, eating area, and other creature comforts
- ❯ reserve a campsite with shade

Entry 32
FINE FEATHERED FRIENDS

As the traveler who has once been from home
is wiser than he who has never left his own doorstep,
so a knowledge of one other culture should
sharpen our ability to scrutinize more steadily,
to appreciate more lovingly, our own.

MARGARET MEAD

There are two basic characteristics of a happy camper: They love people and they love nature. Oh, there are probably camping aficionados out there who wouldn't agree with that—but are they happy? And if they don't love people and nature, why are they camping?

One camping activity that we especially enjoy is bird-watching.

Now, don't get me wrong. We're not out there trying to intentionally spot and identify various bird species or able to identify bird calls. But when we see birds, we take notice. Mostly for our own enjoyment. We always have binoculars in the RV, as well as a bird identification book. Okay, we also have a book with recorded bird calls (at home). But I still wouldn't call us official bird-watchers. Not yet anyway.

I love the sound of a woodpecker tapping away in the woods. Busy at work, they're a gentle reminder that we are inhabiting their world. And there's nothing like seeing a pair of downy woodpeckers taking turns caring for their babies. We even get to peek into the nest the parent birds created in a hollowed-out knothole of an aspen tree. We stay for only a moment, but the image of those fuzzy little birds, chattering away, is unforgettable.

Then there are the elegant pelicans that fly in perfect formation, gracefully floating like a gentle wave over the ocean's surface. It's like an artfully choreographed ballet. But have you ever seen a pelican on land? They're an awkward, almost comical-looking bird. Oh, but when they fly…it's magical.

I love the sound of a hoot owl at night. Five hoots from one direction, answered by five different ones from another area. It's hauntingly beautiful. Another reminder that we are guests in their woods tonight. We also love spotting hawks, eagles, osprey, and golden eagles. One favorite memory is of a pair of red-tailed hawks playfully dropping pinecone bombs on each other—just for the fun of it.

Even camp robbers (like jaybirds) can be entertaining. Not only are they accustomed to human invasions of their territory, they've learned to make the best of it. Leave food unattended for even a minute or two, and you might become host to a friendly camp robber.

One of our favorite experiences with our fine feathered friends involves camping near a coastal estuary. Sitting in our camp chairs at the end of the day, we are gazing out on the peaceful tidal river when we spot a great blue heron soaring directly toward us. We silently watch and wait as the giant bird gracefully lands in a nearby tree. Then we spot another heron doing the same thing. Chris dashes into the RV for binoculars. While he's gone, another heron arrives. We take turns with the binoculars, watching in amazement as about a dozen herons swoop in. And as we take a closer look at the nearby stand of coastal pines, we spot even more herons tucked into the trees. Our final count is more than 20! For the next few days, we pay close attention to our neighbors. By the time we leave, we feel we've made some real fine feathered friends!

But what I probably love most about bird-watching is being reminded of Jesus's words (in Matthew 6:26). He points out that birds aren't farmers and don't store up food, but they always have what they need. So why should we worry? Our heavenly Father will provide for us as well.

You lose sight of things...and when you travel,
everything balances out.
DARANNA GIDEL

TIP FOR THE DAY

Even if you're not a serious bird-watcher, consider packing a small set of good binoculars and
a bird-identifying book. It can be surprisingly
fun. List the unusual birds you spot, including
the date and location.

SPRING IN THE SPRINGS

The ultimate measure of a man is not where
he stands in moments of comfort and convenience,
but where he stands at times of challenge and controversy.

MARTIN LUTHER KING JR.

Living and camping in places where it can freeze in the summertime, we understand the importance of camping rigs that can stand up to the climate. We've learned some little winter tricks, like pouring a bit of antifreeze down the drains, or even leaving a bit of heat on during the extremely cold temps. And, after our plumbing incident in the vineyard campground, our motor home has been completely replumbed with frost-proof pipes. So our plumbing worries are over, right?

As we prepare for a big trip, we check and recheck the motor home to ensure that everything is working and functional. Then we head out. Our destination is Colorado Springs, where I plan to attend a writers' retreat. We hope to enjoy numerous stops and sights along the way. I've made reservations at our final destination, because I've heard that Colorado Springs can be busy around Labor Day. But we're not too concerned about finding campground spaces while we're en route—we'll just take what we get, and everything will work out. Our traveling pace is relaxed and pleasant, and our dependable old Bounder performs as well as ever.

We camp our way through Oregon, Idaho, and Wyoming and finally arrive in Colorado, hoping to settle in before dark. But we haven't counted on Denver traffic. We reach the big city during a thunderstorm and rush hour. The multilane freeway is bumper-to-bumper and barely moving. But we take this in stride, and since we spend most of the time immobilized, I fix us an early dinner. We munch on fruit, cold cuts, cheese, and crackers as we take in the sights of the big city. We thank our lucky stars (and God!) that we don't live in this bustling metropolis.

It's just getting dusky when we reach Colorado Springs, but we quickly find our campground. The place was recommended by friends who live in the Springs, but they've never camped here. Why would they? They live here.

To our dismay, the place looks sketchy. Not exactly a campground, it's more like a rundown mobile home court. Plus, thanks to the rain, the unpaved roads are muddy and messy. To make matters worse, two police cars are parked at the entrance.

I call the office and cancel our reservation. The woman asks why, and I explain that we want to find a different campground. "Everything in the Springs is full," she informs me, a bit smugly. Even so, I cancel our reservation. Then I start to search on my phone. After several calls,

I realize the woman was right. Campgrounds are full. Feeling a little desperate, I pray, asking God to give us a place to stay. Then I call one more number. To my delight, we discover they just had a cancellation, and the spot is ours.

We drive over to the Garden of the Gods area and find the campground. Even though it's dark now, thanks to good lighting, we can see that this is a lovely campground. We settle into our campsite and get everything hooked up. Then we take a walk to admire the great place we've landed in. We couldn't be more pleased. It's perfect.

Worn out from a long day of driving, and knowing that tomorrow will be busy, we go to bed early. Soon, a loud noise wakes me, and I get up to see what it is. Seeing nothing, I sit on our sofa for a bit, listening to the rain. Then I glance out the window to see that it's *not* raining. Our motor home seems to have sprung a leak. Water is gushing from our rig—like a huge sprinkler. I run outside in my PJs and turn off the hose connection. But instead of waking Chris, I go back to bed. We will deal with it tomorrow. Sure, we don't have running water, but at least we're in a delightful location. And instead of trying to resolve the plumbing issue, which appears to be deep inside our rig, we let it go. We pull out our water containers and remember our pioneer ancestors. We're determined to make the best of it. And despite springing a leak, we have a wonderful time in the Springs.

> I guess I just like to challenge myself and push
> myself harder to do things I don't think I can,
> to do things that other people do not think I can.
> It pushes me. I push my own personal limits.
>
> BETHANY HAMILTON

TIP FOR THE DAY

You never know when you'll be deprived of running water. Always carry a spare water container or two—or three. It also helps to have hand sanitizer, wet wipes, and a spray bottle filled with water.

Entry 34

CAMP FRIENDS FOREVER

Perhaps travel cannot prevent bigotry,
but by demonstrating that all peoples cry,
laugh, eat, worry, and die,
it can introduce the idea that if we try
and understand each other,
we may even become friends.

MAYA ANGELOU

If you stay in a campground long enough, you're bound to make new friends. Well, unless you're a bona fide hermit. In that case, you might want to avoid campgrounds altogether. Even backpack camping can turn into a social affair in certain areas. We have found that most campers are rather outgoing. Due to my vocation, I am something of a hermit—but not by choice. It's simply that writing is a rather solitary profession. Probably just one more reason I enjoy camping—it forces me out of my shell.

Even so, I can admit that I sometimes experience culture shock during our first night in a campground. It takes a while for me to get used to neighbors only a few feet away. And because our home's in a quiet neighborhood, I have to adjust myself to the new noises that go together with a campground. But it doesn't take long to get acclimated. And since I'm a wannabe social anthropologist (a side effect of writing), I quickly become curious about my fellow campers. We can see by the variety of license plates that they're from many different states. But what brought them here? Where are they going next? What do they do for a living—or for fun? For my husband and me, connecting with other campers is part of the adventure.

Fellow campers are great resources too. I like hearing their stories—perhaps they'll help inspire characters for my novels. Meanwhile, Chris is great at collecting and sharing camp information. Like "Did you see that eagle's nest?" or "Where did you catch that fish?" They can also recommend campgrounds and restaurants and sights to see—all across the country. And it's always interesting to learn more about points of interest in others' neck of the woods.

I have a theory that we tend to meet the most interesting people in the most interesting campgrounds. Maybe it's because we share common interests. We appreciate nature and wildlife and beautiful locales. This has been a common occurrence at one of our all-time favorite home-state spots. This small campground has a spectacular ocean view.

Since this campground was always in big demand, we'd reserve a "front row" spot well in advance, and sometimes we'd stay there for a week or two. After a four-hour drive, we'd park our motor home facing toward the ocean. We'd just sit there in our cab seats, staring out at the big beautiful sea. No matter the weather, it was always worth the trip. And the sunsets were spectacular. We weren't the only ones who felt that way about this magical spot. In fact, we would often cross paths with old friends, and meet new ones. It felt like going home.

Unfortunately, this campground was such a delightful place that a big East Coast corporation purchased the whole thing and turned it into a fancy expensive members-only private campground. We were not happy campers when we heard about this new development.

Still, we have fond memories of that campground and the campground friends we made (and reunited with) there. Surprisingly, we still cross paths with some of them. I recently met up with some fellow campers while doing a book signing. I didn't recognize them at first, but as soon as they mentioned the campground, it all came back. We talked and laughed and reconnected—like old friends.

We commiserated over the loss of the beautiful campground and shared ideas and suggestions for alternative campgrounds. And I was reminded again that campground friendships are lasting friendships.

You don't have to say everything to be a light.
Sometimes a fire built on a hill will bring
interested people to your campfire.
SHANNON L. ALDER

TIP FOR THE DAY

Not all campgrounds are well-lit or have electric hookups, but solar lights (the kind you can use in your yard at home) come in handy. Whether you choose hanging lanterns to suspend from your awning or a shepherd's hook, or the kind you stake into the ground, they can make your campsite safer and friendlier at night.

THE MORE THE MERRIER

If having a soul means being able
to feel love and loyalty and gratitude,
then animals are better off than a lot of humans.

JAMES HERRIOT

From my childhood, I can recall my mother going on only one camping trip with us. And I must admit that it was a doozy. I don't know if I'd have been a very good sport under the same conditions. And I suppose it helps to explain my mom's reluctance to camp much—especially after *that* trip. In fact, I wonder how we ever talked her into it in the first place. Perhaps it seemed more appealing than staying home and caring for all our pets.

Thanks to my sister's and my love for animals, we always had plenty of them. Despite living in a small house with a tiny yard, we had cats, dogs, chickens, guinea pigs, hamsters, goldfish, and a bird. Maybe I forgot something. Oh, yeah, we had a big white rabbit too. Until he ran away. He probably didn't like living in a zoo.

But suddenly it's summer and our grandparents want to meet up with us for some beach camping. Somehow they assure our mother that we can all fit in their tiny homemade trailer. So we load up our Pontiac with our bags and our pets—which cannot be left home alone—and head out. Our current pet list consists of two guinea pigs (Jose and Honeybun), one recently adopted cat named Muzzy, and a cockapoo named Pandy (along with her four adorable puppies). At this time, we no longer have the bird (thanks to Muzzy) and the goldfish will be okay on their own for a few days. Still, we are like a traveling circus.

When we arrive, our grandparents don't seem overly concerned about our menagerie—or the size of their trailer. Somehow we find spots for everyone. The guinea pigs camp under the trailer, along with the box of puppies, which Pandy keeps a close watch on. Muzzy, who is quite independent, can roam freely. If she wanders too far, my sister and I take turns tracking her down. I think other campers are amused by the big seal-point Siamese cat who acts like she owns the campground.

It's not too bad during the day, but the trailer gets pretty cozy at night. Especially since my sister and I insist on having Muzzy sleep with us. So, my mom, my sister, and I share a bed with Muzzy. It's a wonder anyone gets any sleep.

During the day, my sister and I handle our usual chores of caring for our pets. Our campsite is probably the talk of the campground. There are curious passersby—who probably think we're certifiably nuts. And then there are friendlier folks who appear to be animal lovers too. They stop and pet the big friendly cat and examine the cute puppies. They seem to appreciate the fact that the grownups allowed two little girls to bring all their animal friends camping with them.

What still amazes me is that my grandparents, who have no pets, seem to take all these animals in stride. Grandma even has a sense of humor about it. They seem to enjoy the animals. My grandpa even talks about adopting one of the puppies. All in all, we have a fun—and very memorable—camping trip.

It takes nothing away from a human
to be kind to an animal.

JOAQUIN PHOENIX

TIP FOR THE DAY

When camping with pets, remember to:

> ❯ abide by campground rules

> ❯ avoid leaving pet food where it will attract uninvited wildlife guests (skunks, raccoons, squirrels, chipmunks, etc.)

> ❯ avoid leaving your pet(s) unattended

> ❯ be courteous to fellow campers

> ❯ make sure the campsite is safe for your pet(s)

COWBOY CAMPING

The trail is the thing, not the end of the trail.
Travel too fast and you miss all you are traveling for.
LOUIS L'AMOUR

My husband has never owned a horse, but he has always dreamed of being a cowboy. For the record, Chris was the teenager who wore cowboy boots when everyone else wore sneakers. He had a shearling coat, a Stetson hat, a good hunting rifle, and an old pickup truck. And his favorite author was Louis L'Amour.

So when Chris's buddy wants to go hunting in a very remote and unpopulated region of southeastern Oregon—real cowboy country—Chris is all in. Since the hunting trip involves spending the night—and since these guys are barely 20 at the time—they are ready to rough it. No tent, no trailer, no accommodations. They will do this adventure just like real cowboys.

Their plan is to hunt during the day and to camp out and cook over a campfire at night. And these wannabe cowboys will sleep in the bed of Chris's old Chevy truck, then get up with the sun and do it all over again. I'm sure they see themselves living out a scene in some Clint Eastwood cowboy movie—minus the horses and cattle.

Because it's late autumn, the guys realize it could be chilly out on the lone prairie. Their plan for staying warm at night includes a couple bales of hay and down sleeping bags. Isn't that how a real cowboy would do it? So with their hay bales and camp gear in the back of the truck, these guys set out for adventure.

Although I've heard this tale a few times, I still can't recall what they were hunting for, or if they got anything. I think the only thing Chris remembers from this trip is nearly getting hypothermia.

After a long day of hunting (or playing cowboy), the guys cut open those hay bales, fluffing out that loose hay in the bed of the pickup. Sounds comfy-cozy, right? Apparently not. Although they try to burrow their sleeping bags down into the hay, the temperature keeps plunging until it's freezing cold out. It probably doesn't help that the pickup bed is metal with cold air flowing beneath and around it. The "cowboys" would have fared better if they'd slept on the ground next to the campfire.

Finally, they're shivering and shaking and can no longer stand the cold. These big, rough and tough men get into the pickup cab, turn on the engine and heater, and attempt to thaw out. Because they're so far off the beaten path, there's no hotel, motel, or hostel nearby. No refuge to seek warmth or shelter. And so, cutting their losses, the weary weekend warriors head for home in the middle of the night.

I guess I should be thankful for the lesson Chris learned from that trip—and a number of other less-than-comfortable camping experiences. *Don't go out unless you're well-prepared for the elements.* After all, there's nothing wrong with camping in warmth and comfort.

We have a sense that we should be like the mythical cowboy...able to take on and conquer anything and live in the world without the need for other people.

MORRIE SCHWARTZ

TIP FOR THE DAY

You don't have to be a cowboy to appreciate some of their tools. A good cowboy hat is great for camping, a horse blanket makes a good bench warmer, a canteen keeps drinking water cool, and singing 'round the campfire makes for happy campers.

Entry 37

THE KISSING BEAR

The world of life, of spontaneity,
the world of dawn and sunset and starlight,
the world of soil and sunshine, of meadow and woodland,
of hickory and oak and maple and hemlock
and pineland forests, of wildlife dwelling around us,
of the river and its well-being—
all of this is the integral community in which we live.

THOMAS BERRY

Not many sights are as beautiful as the Teton Mountains in June. After camping in Yellowstone for a few days, we realize we don't have sufficient time to stay overnight in Grand Teton National Park on this leg of our journey. Our schedule forces us to keep moving, but we take our time as we drive through the gorgeous national park. We stop many times on the way.

We're on the lookout for wildlife as we go. Particularly
for bears. We've heard they're here in numbers right now.
And because we didn't see many bears in Yellowstone, we
hope to spy one or two here. As we're driving around
the ridge of Jackson Lake, I see something interesting.
"Down there," I tell Chris. "Bear!"

He pulls over so we can get a better look. Sure enough, we see not one but
two bears meandering around the lake's beachside edge. They are golden brown,
and, from our higher viewpoint, appear smaller than they are. We watch the two
bears with fascination.

"Hey, there's another bear." I point down to a golden-brown figure not too
far from the pair of bears. "It's lying down."

Chris follows my gaze, then looks alarmed. "That's not a bear!" He starts the
pickup again, heading down the road. "That's a person!"

I look more closely as he drives, realizing Chris is right. What I assumed
was a bear is really a curvy woman who appears to be sunbathing—completely
oblivious to the bears coming directly her way! "Hurry," I tell Chris. "The bears
are getting closer!"

We come to a pullout right above the trailhead, which leads down to that
section of beach. We both jump out of the truck. Chris moves to warn the sun-
bather about the approaching bears. But he's barely on the trail when a sun-
tanned woman in a swimsuit comes racing up.

"The bear licked me," she screams.

"What happened?" we ask, trying to calm her.

"The bear—it came right to me," she gasps. "It rifled through my stuff. It ate my potato chips—and then it licked me!" She is crying now.

We reassure her that it'll be okay and that she's safe. And, making light of her experience, I jokingly suggest that the bear just wanted to kiss her. "It's a kissing bear," I say.

Now she remembers that all her stuff is still down on the beach. "My purse and car keys and everything." She shakes her head. "But I can't go back down there."

Chris heroically offers to go down and get her things. I warn him to be very careful, and he promises he will. Meanwhile, I try to calm and comfort the rattled woman. She tells me that she works at the lodge and that employees have been warned to be on the lookout for bears. "I feel so stupid for being down there," she says.

"Well, at least you have a story to tell now," I tell her. "You've been kissed by a bear. Not everyone can make that claim."

She starts to grasp this and eventually laughs about it. Chris returns in one piece with her things, and she is very grateful. We visit with her awhile, making sure she's calm enough to drive her car. She thanks us again. We wish her well and part ways. And despite not getting to actually camp in Grand Teton National Park that time, we leave with a lasting memory.

Man has been driven out of the paradise
in which he could trust his instincts.

KONRAD LORENZ

TIP FOR THE DAY

Before your next camping trip, research the best ways to avoid or deal with a close encounter with a wild animal. Remember, all animals react differently. What works for a cougar doesn't necessarily work for a bear.

Entry 38
GIRL TRIP

Just try new things. Don't be afraid.
Step out of your comfort zones and soar, all right?

MICHELLE OBAMA

My sister and I have both tried to reform our mother into a more outdoorsy woman. We've attempted to gently introduce her to camping—with the comforts that we've learned to embrace. And it does seem that she's made progress. But when I suggest that my sister and I meet up with Mom for her birthday at a midway campground, she doesn't sound enthusiastic.

I tell her we'll be staying in the motor home, which is pretty comfortable. I describe the campground to her—the wonderful hot-spring pools and the beautiful gardens nearby. I explain how it's become a favorite getaway spot for Chris and me—and that there are a few good restaurants nearby. "It's luxurious camping," I assure her. "We'll do everything to make you comfortable. It'll be fun."

And so she agrees. Albeit reluctantly. So now the pressure is on. I make our reservation and confirm the plan with my sister. I am resolved to make this girls' getaway great. Never mind that I've never driven and set up the motor home on my own. Oh, I can drive it all right. But I've never gone on a trip without Chris there to help. And the truth is that he does most of the work.

Naturally, my concerned husband questions if I'm really up for this challenge. He reminds me that the motor home is big, and setting up is work. But I assure him I can do it. Even so, we go over the steps for everything. From remembering to set the parking brake to how to connect to water and electric. I think he's rather amused and probably expects me to beg him to play chauffeur at the last minute. After all, we could tow the Jeep and he could drive it back home, then return to pick us up later. But that seems like a lot of unnecessary work. And my plan is to drive without a tow vehicle—to do it all myself. It'll be a good lesson.

Soon, my sister and I are on our way. Behind the wheel of our motor home, I remind myself, "I can do this."

The drive is smooth. When we get to the campground, I discover that we have a riverside campsite, and I'll need to back the RV into it. Backing up has never been my strong suit. It doesn't help that the back of our campsite is a drop-off into the river. If I back up too far.... Well, we don't want to go there.

With the help of my sis—and a silent prayer—I manage to get the RV safely into place. I set the parking brake. Then we work together to get it all hooked up and prepare our campsite. Then, feeling like can-do frontier women, we wait for our mom to arrive.

I can't speak for my mom and sister, but I thoroughly enjoyed that girls-only camping trip. Maybe I was simply relieved that we arrived and parked safely—without landing in the river. For the next two days, we soaked in the hot springs, walked through the gardens, enjoyed the lodge, visited by the campfire, played cards, ate good food, and slept comfortably. Most of all, we enjoyed being together. And, really, what could be better than that?

You will never be completely at home again,
Because part of your heart always will be elsewhere.
That is the price you pay for the richness of loving
and knowing people in more than one place.
MIRIAM ADENEY

TIP FOR THE DAY

Make fire-starters by filling egg-carton "holes" with melted wax (from old leftover candles). Tear off a single egg section, nest it in the kindling, and light the egg-carton paper on fire for a quick, easy campfire.

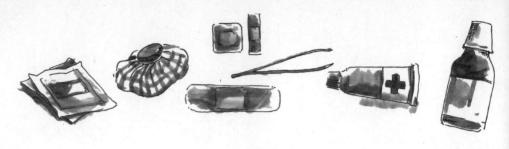

READY FOR ANYTHING

If you don't go after what you want, you'll never have it.
If you don't ask, the answer is always no.
If you don't step forward, you are always in the same place.

NORA ROBERTS

Because we live in forest-fire country, I often refer to our motor home as our mobile emergency kit. That's because it's always equipped with clothing, bedding, first aid supplies, drinking water, basic food staples, and survival tools... anything and everything you could possibly need in the state of a real emergency or natural disaster. And enough to share with others too. We even keep it stocked with things like toothpaste and shampoo.

During fire season, we also make sure the RV is filled with gas, propane, and fresh water. And we keep it headed out of the driveway. One year, when we lived right next to the national forest and were on level-two evacuation alert, we even loaded the Bounder with those irreplaceable items we wouldn't want to lose if a fire destroyed our home. We kept tuned to the news and remained ready to roll.

Fortunately, we didn't have to make a run-for-your-life escape. Now that we've moved into town, we hope we never will. But it's reassuring to know the RV is good to go at any given moment. That's one of the side benefits of being a campy person. It's kind of like being a Boy Scout—you try to be prepared for anything. Of course, that also makes it easier to go camping on short notice. And I love the idea of spur-of-the-moment getaways.

Sometimes all we need to motivate us to take an impromptu camping trip is a weather report. For instance, it can be the never-ending winter here in the mountains but springlike on the other side. What more motivation do you need?

Late summer is notorious for wildfires where we live. And sometimes the smoke isn't just ugly; it's unsafe. One August morning we wake to heavy smoke, so thick we can barely see across the street. Not only that, but it's stinking hot. Time to get out of town.

We grab a few perishables from the fridge—and the dog—then lock up and hop into the motor home and take off. We're not sure of our final destination yet, but we are headed west, and our goal is to find a smoke-free campground. Well, unless it's campfire smoke. Driving through our smoked-out town, we feel sorry for those who are stuck here. We hope they can stay inside, with AC to keep them cool.

Because the West seems riddled with wildfires, we drive until we reach the coast. We're not sure where we'll find an available campsite, whether it's an RV park, roadside state park, or even the casino where "camping" is free—we don't really care. We're just glad to be here.

When we step out of the RV, it's almost shocking. The sea breeze is blowing, the fog is rolling in off the ocean, and the temperature is nearly 40 degrees colder than home. It's all just perfectly delicious. It feels delightful to pull on a sweatshirt and wear socks again. Even the dog is thrilled at the cooler environment. It's like we've entered a different world. Everything feels fresh and new and good.

Sure, our lives probably weren't in actual danger from the smoke and heat, but it feels like our mobile emergency kit has saved us, and we are grateful for the escape.

I'm an idealist. I don't know where
I'm going, but I'm on my way.

CARL SANDGUR

TIP FOR THE DAY

When making an unexpected getaway, you can't always assume that an electronic GPS or phone will get you where you're going. That's why you need a good road map. And if you like to hike and explore new territory, learn how to mark a trail, to read a map, and, most important, how to use a compass.

ON THE BEACH

The world is round and the place which may seem
like the end may also be the beginning.

IVY BAKER PRIEST

The beach is one of our favorite places to camp. While we owned a beach cabin, we didn't need to drive our RV over to enjoy the seaside. For about eight years, we "camped" in our tiny cabin, becoming so familiar with that area of coastline that we felt completely at home there. But that all changed a few years ago. Although it was hard to let the beach cabin go, it was time. Now we're redis-covering how fun it is to camp at new places up and down the Pacific coastline.

But one of our favorite on-the-beach memories occurred at our beach cabin—at Christmastime. It was also the inspiration for one of my Christmas novellas (*A Christmas by the Sea*).

It's December and because other family members have other plans, Chris

and I decide to spend the holidays at our cabin. This is a first, but we're looking forward to it. But when we get a beautiful noble fir that takes up half of our sunroom, I realize I don't have any-thing to decorate it with. Because everything in our cabin is very coastal looking, I decide to continue this theme on the tree. I find a few things that seem to work, but the big tree still looks a bit bare. At the end of the day, as we're walking along the beach, we're surprised to find several unbroken sand dollars. After years of looking, we've found only seven whole sand dollars.

That night, there's a storm and, according to our tide table, tomorrow morning is a minus tide. Ideal conditions for shell seeking. We agree to get up early, hoping to find a few more sand dollars or some other interesting shells that can be transformed into tree ornaments. The next morning, with bread bags in our parka pockets, we pull on our Bogs boots and hit the beach—hoping to get lucky.

Wading in the ankle-deep water, we immediately begin to find whole sand dollars. Lots and lots of sand dollars! We can't believe it—it's like winning the sand dollar lottery. We see a few other beachcombers strolling along, but no one else is down here by the water line, capitalizing on the abundance of these amazing sand dollars. We joke that we're sand dollar pirates—gathering our bounty.

Eventually the tide comes in and there seem to be no more sand dollars to be found. That's okay; our bread bags and pockets are heavy with them. So we take our find home and count them. We're stunned to discover we have almost 400! We spend several hours cleaning them and laying them out to dry. That night we go see a local production of *The Nutcracker Suite*—with visions of sand dollars still dancing in our heads.

The next morning, under similar conditions to the previous day, we head back to the beach. We doubt there will be any sand dollars left after the way we cleaned up yesterday. But it happens again. Only today, we find even more! By the time we're done with collecting sand dollars, we have nearly a thousand! That afternoon, after hours of cleaning and drying sand dollars, I start to make ornaments. And then we decorate the tree with dozens of sand dollar "angels."

That evening, we sit and stare at what we both agree is the most beautiful Christmas tree ever!

Every time I stand before a beautiful beach,
Its waves seem to whisper to me:
If you choose the simple things
And find joy in nature's simple treasures,
Life and living need not be so hard.

ROXAS-MENDOZA

TIP FOR THE DAY

How to make sand dollar angels: I use a sand dollar for the body, then hot-glue two small clam shells for wings and a round glass or stone pebble on the top for a head. Hot-glue a looped string on the back for a hanger.

Entry 41

GLAMPING 101

You can't use up creativity.
The more you use, the more you have.

MAYA ANGELOU

Some women question how I can possibly enjoy camping. Isn't it dirty? And uncomfortable? And what about the deprivations out there in the wilderness? That's when I try to enlighten my uninformed female friend about the difference between camping and *glamping*. I don't know who first coined that term (although I'm sure it was a woman), but I can personally attest to the fact that I've been doing it for about 25 years.

I'm sure some of my early camping experiences have contributed to my appreciation of glamping. Getting soaked or chilled, not to mention sleepless nights, is motivation for camping a bit more comfortably. Even more so as I get older.

I don't see why our camping rig couldn't benefit from a few improvements.

Shouldn't it be like a home away from home? So if I enjoy good bedding at home, wouldn't I appreciate it that much more while camping? Who doesn't want a good night's sleep when they're on the road? That's why our RV has a good mattress, nice pillows, a cozy duvet, soft sheets, and a lavender candle to aid relaxation.

But there are many ways to glamp. Different strokes for different folks. It might be a quality sleeping bag, a cute kerosene lamp, and a charming set of enamelware. Maybe it's having a well-equipped kitchen and making fabulous food. Perhaps it's a camp wardrobe that, while practical, still makes you feel good. It can be something as simple as arranging pretty wildflowers in an old canning jar, or spreading some colorful autumn leaves on your picnic table before a meal. It's like being kind to yourself—and what's wrong with that?

Glamping, to me, is making your camping experience comfortable and appealing—and attractive, according to your sense of style. Of course, that means you need to consider your preferred method of camping. If you're a tent camper, you probably won't be packing percale sheets and fine china. If you camp in a big fancy RV, you probably won't be using a sleeping bag. It's all relative.

I'm sure some people think I go over the top in redecorating and outfitting our camping rigs. But I love doing it. It makes me happy. More importantly, it makes me feel like a trailer or RV is truly *ours*. It makes me feel at home. We've had our motor home for almost two decades, and I'm sure most people would be surprised at all I've done to transform its decor over the years. If I had to describe the style of our RV, it's sort of lodge with touches of Pendleton.

Besides reupholstering, I've changed wallpaper borders, painted walls, switched out cabinet hardware, replaced lampshades, added wood blinds, and re-covered valances. I've also added family photos and artwork that has meaning to us. Every piece I bring into our RV is intentional. I ask two questions: Do I love it? Is it useful?

My RV is not the place for castoffs. Whether its towels or dishes or hiking shoes, I don't want to waste any precious space with items I don't like or use.

Over the years, we've also replaced our cab chairs, fridge, table, and a few other important pieces—including the toilet. We've made that RV our own. Every time we go out in it, we feel like we're in our home away from home. To me, that's really glamping.

Great things are not done by impulse,
but a series of small things brought together.
VINCENT VAN GOGH

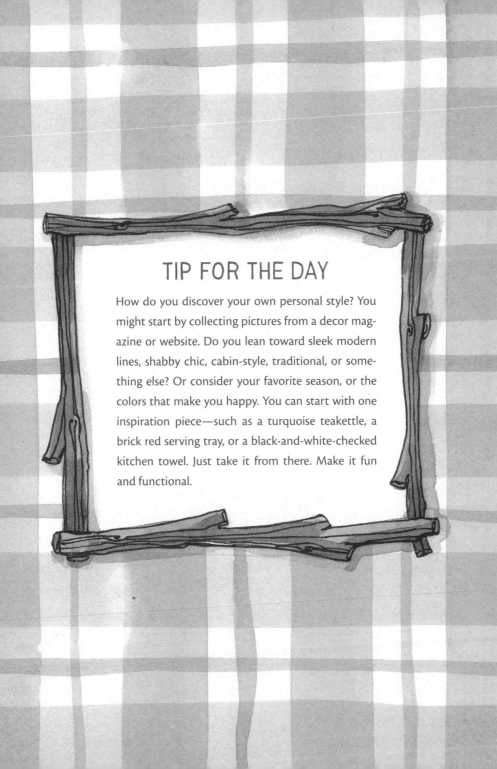

TIP FOR THE DAY

How do you discover your own personal style? You might start by collecting pictures from a decor magazine or website. Do you lean toward sleek modern lines, shabby chic, cabin-style, traditional, or something else? Or consider your favorite season, or the colors that make you happy. You can start with one inspiration piece—such as a turquoise teakettle, a brick red serving tray, or a black-and-white-checked kitchen towel. Just take it from there. Make it fun and functional.

Entry 42

ONE FISH, TWO FISH

Fishing is much more than fish.
It is the great occasion when we may return
to the fine simplicity of our forefathers.

HERBERT HOOVER

My grandpa loved to go fishing. Sometimes he went out on the ocean, sometimes in a river or creek, and sometimes on a lake. Because I loved my grandpa and loved the same things he loved (like pancakes and building things and going to the hardware store), I felt certain I would love fishing too. Especially considering that, although I was a picky eater, I liked to eat fish. So I could hardly wait to go fishing with Grandpa. Even though I'd never done it, I was certain I would love it.

I'm about six or seven the first time I get an opportunity to go fishing. My grandparents and I are camping at a good fishing lake when Grandpa invites me to go out with him, early in the morning the next day. Of course I eagerly say yes!

I'm so excited that I can barely sleep that night. Grandpa has already warned me that we'll be out on the lake for a while and that I'll have to be patient. But I have assured him that will be just fine with me. He also told me I'll have to be quiet, because we don't want to scare off the fish. Again, I agreed. I might be a kid, but I am good at being quiet.

Early in the morning, with our brown-bag breakfasts in hand, we set out in his aluminum boat. The small outboard engine chugs happily, moving us to the side of the lake where Grandpa says the fishing is better.

I sit quietly in the rear of the boat, watching in silent fascination as Grandpa rolls some Velveeta cheese into tiny balls. He puts a couple of these orange balls onto his hook, then lowers it into the water, with a twinkle in his blue eyes. I want to ask him if the fish like cheese, but I'm trying to remain quiet. Before long, he is reeling in his line. Then I watch with wide-eyed wonder as he removes a wriggling fish, tossing it into the wooden box behind me.

He repeats this process and, shortly after he lowers his line, there's another tug. He reels in another fish and tosses it into the box. And it's not that I'm bored with watching him catch these fish, but the noise in the box behind me is distracting. So while he's baiting his hook, I turn to see that some of the fish are very much alive. And they don't look too happy.

I reach into the wooden box and scoop up a particularly lively fish and, while

Grandpa is lowering his hook, I drop the fish back into the water. I feel slightly guilty as I do this, but I think the fish appreciates it. And while Grandpa is occupied with fishing, I free a few more fish.

When Grandpa catches me in the act of releasing a fish, he doesn't scold me, but he asks why I've done that. I sheepishly confess I feel sorry for the fish. He quietly informs me the fish I released will most likely die anyway, because they have been out of the water too long. Although I'm not so sure about that, I understand that what I did was wrong. After all, we came out here to fish—and I agreed to Grandpa's terms.

I don't free any more fish after that. When it's time for dinner that evening, and my grandma cooks up some delicious trout, I partake as usual. And I'm grateful...both for the meal and for my first fishing lesson with Grandpa.

> Look at where Jesus went to pick people.
> He didn't go to the colleges;
> he got guys off the fishing docks.
>
> JEFF FOXWORTHY

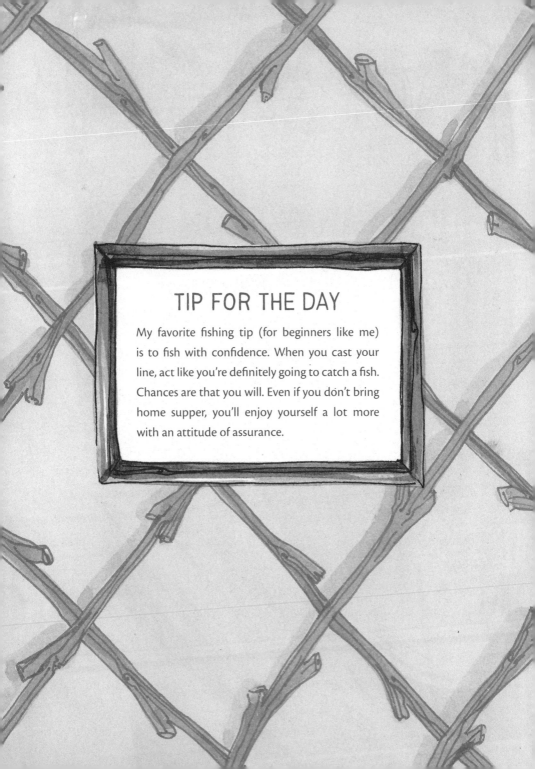

TIP FOR THE DAY

My favorite fishing tip (for beginners like me) is to fish with confidence. When you cast your line, act like you're definitely going to catch a fish. Chances are that you will. Even if you don't bring home supper, you'll enjoy yourself a lot more with an attitude of assurance.

Entry 43

HOME AWAY FROM HOME

Each day is a journey,
and the journey itself is home.

MATSUO BASHO

When my husband's mother was facing the end of life and his father needed to move into assisted living, we wanted to be nearby to help. But they were far enough away to make daily trips inconvenient. Because we didn't want to stay in a hotel, we decided to take our motor home over the mountain and park it nearby.

Because it's wintertime, reserving a campsite is easy. We locate an attractive RV park next to the river and, although the circumstances are sad, it's a comfort to camp next to a peaceful view. We set up camp as usual, trying to make ourselves at home.

Our daytime is split between visiting Chris's two parents—driving back and forth between the nursing home and the assisted-living complex. We try to comfort Chris's mom in her final days and help Chris's dad get settled into his new accommodations. They are both in such need, and we're glad we can be around to lend a hand.

But by the end of the day, we go home to our RV, feeling weary and worn out…and sad. We fix ourselves dinner and talk about the situation, trying to determine what we can do to help his parents make these difficult life adjustments. The next day, we do it all again.

After a couple of days, we realize that there's really little we can do besides being supportive and understanding with Chris's parents. As much as we love them, we can't change their situation or circumstances. It's just life, the end of life. It's not easy—for any of us.

Still, after a long day, it's a relief to return to our home away from home. And sitting outside, watching the river, talking about the day, enjoying the peace and quiet…it somehow helps. Sure, it's not a fun camping trip, but it's better than staying in a hotel. Not to mention the money we're saving. Or that we can sleep better here. Being able to prepare our own food feels healthier, and it saves a few bucks too.

So we're grateful, in a whole new way, for our well-equipped RV. In a small but big way, it's making a difficult situation better for us. We hope we're making things better for Chris's parents as well. I'm relieved that Chris is getting the chance to be with his parents and to say his final goodbyes—before they go on to their next home.

This is a reminder to us that we are getting older too. Someday we'll be in a similar place. Oh, it's hard to imagine it now, but we know it's inevitable. As a result, it makes us more resolved to make the most of this life while we have it. For us, that means many things, including more camping trips, making new friends, having more adventures, interacting with nature…and with each other.

I know that Chris's parents would appreciate that. After all, they enjoyed similar activities. From adventures in their little camp trailer, rock-hounding, discovering out-of-the-way places…to meeting interesting people, it's a legacy we're happy to receive from them.

We hope we'll pass it along to the next generation.

The ache for home lives in all of us,
the safe place where we can go as we are
and not be questioned.

MAYA ANGELOU

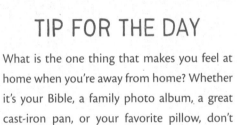

TIP FOR THE DAY

What is the one thing that makes you feel at home when you're away from home? Whether it's your Bible, a family photo album, a great cast-iron pan, or your favorite pillow, don't leave home without it.

Entry 44

OUTDOOR DECOR

We travel not to escape life, but for life not to escape us.

AUTHOR UNKNOWN

Every campground usually has one—unless there are restrictions: I'm guessing you've seen an overly flamboyant campsite before. The one that resembles a psychedelic yard sale, on steroids. A small area with a few too many bright banners, whirligigs, goofy signs, colored lights, fake flowers, and pink flamingos. You get the picture. It's not the campsite people want to park next to. It's not because these happy campers aren't nice. These fun-loving folks tend to be full-timers with a penchant for collecting funky stuff. If you take the time, they usually have interesting tales to tell.

While I support every camper's right to express individuality—and I personally love to create outdoor spaces that make me feel at home and happy—I believe that less is more. In the same way that fashion needs editing, some kitschy campsites could probably use a little editing too. I realize we campers love the free feeling of hitting the road and enjoying some liberating downtime, but sometimes we need a reminder that we're sharing the campground with others. So whether it's overly loud speakers, pesky pets, a disregard for campsite boundaries, or an overly cluttered campsite, we all need to respect our fellow campers.

But that doesn't mean you should have a bare-bones, plain-Jane campsite. After all, camping's supposed to be fun, right? So why not give your campsite a little pizzazz and personality? Just don't take it too far.

When we're gone for a week or two, I might take along a pot of geraniums to brighten our "front yard." And I have a string of white lights that I often hang on our awning—especially in winter, when daylight hours are shorter. Sometimes I'll even put out my wind chimes, which are not *too* noisy.

If the campsite outside our door is bare dirt, I'll put out an outdoor carpet. After that, our comfy camp-lounge chairs. Then if it's cool out, I'll toss out a pair of color-coordinated polar fleece throws. Then I'll set up a small folding side table and place a lantern on it. If we're only there for one night, that might be all I do. But we feel at home.

If we're camped for a longer time, I almost always place a pretty tablecloth on the picnic table (I have several to choose from stowed beneath our sofa). Then I'll place several lanterns on the table for night dining and warm ambiance. I also keep matching polar fleece throws on hand to use as bench pads or knee warmers. And I usually have a mason jar of fresh flowers or collected campy foliage as a centerpiece. It just makes me feel at home and happy.

Even when we're gone for the day, I leave all my decor items out. Nothing has ever gone missing. At the end of the day, it's welcoming to come home to a pretty campsite. It also makes it more fun to be hospitable. And because we like inviting others to join us, we always carry extra camp chairs. We take our own fire ring, in case we're camped in a spot without a fire pit (but we always check to be sure a campfire is allowed—and it usually is). How else can you make real s'mores?

There are lots of ways to make your campsite's exterior fun and inviting and, once again, it's a great chance to express your individuality. One trick I learned early on is to consider color when it comes to your camp accessories. Pick a lead color or two that go with the exterior of your camp rig. Then, whether it's chairs, blankets, tablecloths, cookware, or lanterns—if you stay within that color palette, the results will be a coordinated and eye-pleasing campsite. A place you'll be happy to come home to.

In order to create you have to believe in your ability
to do so. And that often means excluding whole
chunks of normal life, and pumping yourself up
as much as possible as a way of keeping on.

T.C. BOYLE

TIP FOR THE DAY

Getting attractive camp accessories doesn't have to break the bank. Garage sales and off-season sales are good ways to find bargains. Flea market items can add color and fun to your outdoor decor too. And never underestimate what an inexpensive cute tablecloth that complements your camp dishware can do to brighten your campsite.

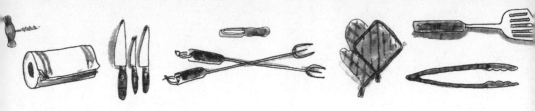

COOKING OUT

Food is our common ground,
a universal experience.

JAMES BEARD

When we got into cast-iron cookware for camping, my husband went all out by getting a wrought-iron tripod. His plan was to set it over a campfire, along with a big black cauldron to hang on it. Kind of like something you'd see outside the chuck wagon on a cattle drive—or something for a witch's brew. Naturally, Chris prefers the cowboy image. But we did put it to use on Halloween one year.

Okay, this isn't exactly a *camping* story (this harvesttime gathering happened at our home), but a lot of people thought our cabin-style home in the woods was pretty campy. And because this get-together over food happened outside, I think it works for this book. Plus, I can't deny that it's probably my all-time favorite outdoor cooking tale. It brought a lot of people together. And that's the best kind of story.

It starts out with a fond childhood memory that Chris has told me about numerous times. On Halloween, when he was a kid, a family in his neighborhood made a big pot of sloppy joes over an open fire and served it to trick-or-treaters. Apparently, Chris loved it so much that he went back for seconds. And thirds.

So we decide to do something like that in our neighborhood. We haven't lived there very long, and it seems like a good way to get to know our neighbors, who all tend to keep to themselves. Especially with winter around the corner.

Chris takes invitations to all the houses in our neighborhood. We assume that maybe a handful, if any, will come. But just in case, we get a ton of hamburger and lots of buns and onions and the rest of the sloppy-joe ingredients. I imagine we'll have leftovers until Christmas.

Trying to get in the spirit of things, I decorate our large covered porch with pumpkins, lanterns, a scarecrow, strings of lights, and so on. Because we live on acre-plus lots, the neighbors aren't very close. As a result, we get few trick-or-treaters. So we haven't really put much effort into Halloween before.

Late in the day, we get the fire going out in the courtyard and, although I help get the ingredients ready, Chris is in charge of cooking the sloppy-joe sauce. It looks like there's enough to feed an army. The aroma is tantalizing, and I wonder if it will entice our neighbors to come. If they do come, will they think it's silly or childish for us to serve sloppy joes?

Not only do they come, but it seems that almost everyone invited shows up! Our porch and courtyard are filled with neighbors. Many, up until now, have never met each other. Now we're all together having fun, and everyone is feasting on sloppy joes. And going back for seconds...and thirds. Then one neighbor asks if her musician sons can come over and bring their band. Suddenly, we have live music—and it's good!

The campfire is like the centerpiece of the gathering, and after the last of the sloppy joes are gone, I set out chocolate bars, marshmallows, and graham crackers. With the musicians still playing and everyone still having a good time, we make s'mores. This evening turns out to be one of those get-togethers that the whole neighborhood talks about for years to come. Strangers who became friends...over something as simple as sloppy joes, music, and s'mores.

If you really want to make a friend,
Go to someone's house and eat with him...
The people who give you their food give you their heart.
CESAR CHAVEZ

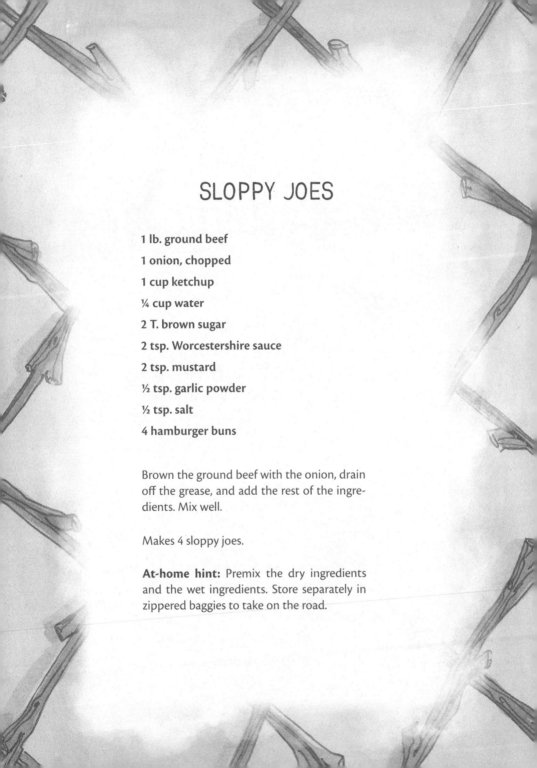

SLOPPY JOES

1 lb. ground beef

1 onion, chopped

1 cup ketchup

¼ cup water

2 T. brown sugar

2 tsp. Worcestershire sauce

2 tsp. mustard

½ tsp. garlic powder

½ tsp. salt

4 hamburger buns

Brown the ground beef with the onion, drain off the grease, and add the rest of the ingredients. Mix well.

Makes 4 sloppy joes.

At-home hint: Premix the dry ingredients and the wet ingredients. Store separately in zippered baggies to take on the road.

THE GIRL SCOUT CABIN

You are not here merely to…make a living.
You are here in order to enable the world
to live more amply, with greater vision,
with a finer spirit of hope and achievement.
You are here to enrich the world, and you
impoverish yourself if you forget the errand.

WOODROW WILSON

About the same time we were renovating our beach cabin, my sister was busily rescuing an old Girl Scout cabin in the mountains. Tucked into the woods, on some property my sister and her husband owned, this tiny, one-room cabin had some great tales to tell about the Girl Scouts who'd camped there in years gone by. Perhaps more importantly, it also had great potential. But to the casual observer it looked like a pack rat–infested shack that might as well be torn down. Just the same, my sister liked it. She could see it had good bones. And so she went to work.

In the next few years, that tiny cabin was completely restored—transformed into something far better than it had ever been before. Now it's a delightful little getaway with so much campy eye-candy that I think it should be featured in a cabin magazine. My sister has decorated with all sorts of vintage items. Everywhere you look, there's something worth seeing. And yet it's comfortable. A perfect mix of fun and functionality.

Every time I've visited there, I have walked around to take it all in. And there's always some new improvement. But it's not just the cabin that makes this place so wonderful. It's the beautiful piney woods around it, the wildflowers growing in the meadow, and the wildlife (including moose, elk, deer) you can spot while you're up there.

Although I've visited the Girl Scout cabin in the daytime, I hadn't stayed overnight up there. Usually because there'd be a conflict in someone's schedule. Finally, I'm visiting my sister for her birthday in October, keeping her company while her husband is elk hunting. So I ask her if we can spend the night up at her cabin. Of course she loves her cabin and doesn't often get anyone who wants to sleep over there, so she eagerly says yes.

As always, the pretty little cabin welcomes us. It's still as cute as can be—even better than I remember. And although it's cold, we soon get the chill off with a rip-roaring fire in the little woodstove. We also make a fire in the outside fire pit. I've never been up there after dark before, but the place looks truly magical with all the lights on and fires going. Very sweet.

We enjoy a nice evening, eating and visiting and catching up. When it's time for bed, I realize I've never been up in the sleeping loft before. A pair of twin beds with attractive campy bedding are nestled into the small loft. But I quickly discover, with a bump to my head, the ceiling is very low up here. Still, the bed is comfortable and by now the whole cabin is toasty warm, and I'm tired. I drift to sleep.

Unfortunately, I've always been a restless sleeper, and I've developed the habit of sitting up in bed to readjust myself and get comfortable. But each time I sit up, still half asleep, I whack my head on the low ceiling. After several startling head bonks, I either knock myself out or figure it out. Somehow, I sleep until morning, waking up with some bumps on my head. Still, I loved spending time with my sister and sleeping overnight at the Girl Scout cabin—but the next time I go, I think I'll pack a helmet!

Consider a tree for a moment. As beautiful as
trees are to look at, we don't see what goes on
underground—as they grow roots.
Trees must develop deep roots in order to grow
strong and produce their beauty. But we don't see
the roots. We just see and enjoy the beauty.
In much the same way, what goes on inside
of us is like the roots of a tree.

JOYCE MEYER

TIP FOR THE DAY

Day-to-day living in a tiny cabin isn't too different from an RV. You learn to respect compact spaces, and you create clever ways to make everything fit. To accomplish that, consider multipurpose items. A bench is not just for sitting; it's for storing shoes and boots. A picnic basket isn't just for outings; it's for stashing table linens and kitchen towels. A vintage tin isn't just eye-candy; it's for tea bags.

Entry 47

INCONVENIENT CONVENIENCES

There are no wrong turnings.
Only paths we had not known we were meant to walk.

GUY GAVRIEL KAY

When taking an extended trip, you sometimes forget to make a reservation. Or you discover a distraction and your driving schedule changes. Or you arrive too late and discover your space has been taken and the campground is full. For whatever reason, you sometimes find yourself sacrificing ambiance for convenience. Maybe you wind up at a big box store with a complimentary RV section, or you park at a highway weigh station that's closed for the night, or you find a "hospitable" casino that welcomes guests with free camping.

While on our way to Montana, we find ourselves in this position. It's getting

late and we've tarried too long on the road. As a result, we
decide to try out a "one-night stand" at an Idaho casino
that offers free campsites. After all, their billboard a
few miles back looked inviting. Never mind that we're
not gamblers. All we want is a good night's sleep—and an early departure the
next morning. This place looks convenient, and the price is right!

The casino turns out to be a group of gigantic tents. Very festive looking,
like a circus. The RV parking area is a muddy field that's surprisingly full, but we
take this as a good sign. It must be a popular place to camp. We find a spot and
settle in. Naturally, there are no hookups. But we don't mind. This is going to
be a quick stopover, and our batteries are charged, our propane and fresh water
tanks are full.

As we prepare dinner, we notice that this place is loud. Not just the camping
area, but the casino as well. But it's still early in the evening. We expect it will
quiet down as bedtime rolls around.

Think again. Instead of quieting down, this place gets louder and louder.
Music blasts from the casino, people laugh and shout and slam RV doors, but
no one goes to bed. It's well past midnight when we hear what sounds like a
serious brawl. Our convenient overnight stop is feeling more like a form of
sleep-deprivation torture.

Somehow, Chris manages to sleep, but in the wee hours of the morning I'm
still wide awake, listening to the cacophony that sounds like it's just outside our
door. By now the partiers out there don't sound like they're having fun. I suspect
some have lost big money at the casino.

When another fight develops—even hotter than the last one—I almost expect to hear gunfire or police sirens. That is, if this area is even serviced by police, which I doubt. Naturally, my imagination is as out of control as these camper-gamblers, who never seem to go to bed.

Finally the sun is coming up and, although I'm bleary eyed and not what you'd call a happy camper, I'm relieved it's morning. I can't wait to escape this torturous place. But surprisingly—or not—the campground and casino are both deathly quiet now. I assume the rabble-rousers from last night finally wore themselves out and crashed. For a brief moment, I consider capitalizing on the silence and returning to bed. But more than I want sleep, I want to escape this place.

Without even fixing breakfast, we pull up our stabilizing jacks, start our engine, and we are out of there. I don't even care that our noise could be disturbing our fellow campers, who are obviously sleeping it off. Lesson learned: A conveniently located and free campground isn't always worth it. Next time, we'll check things out better before sacrificing a good night's sleep.

Nature has been for me, for as long as I remember,
a source of solace, inspiration, adventure, and delight;
a home, a teacher, a companion.
LORRAINE ANDERSON

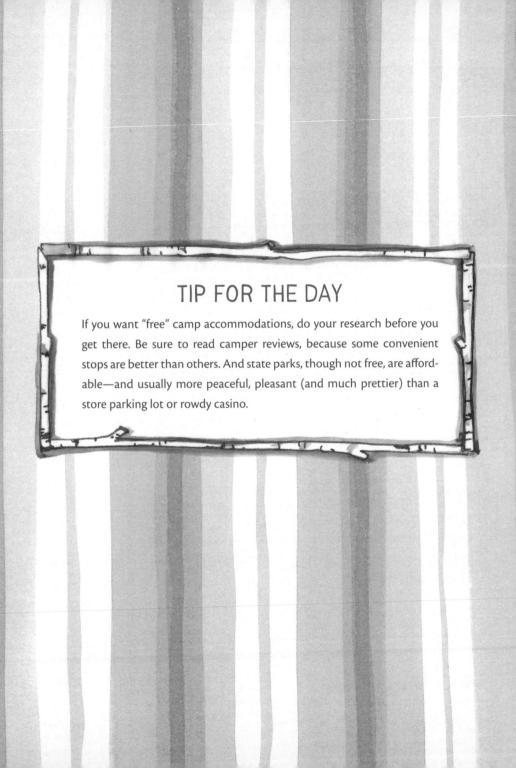

TIP FOR THE DAY

If you want "free" camp accommodations, do your research before you get there. Be sure to read camper reviews, because some convenient stops are better than others. And state parks, though not free, are affordable—and usually more peaceful, pleasant (and much prettier) than a store parking lot or rowdy casino.

LESS IS MORE

The secret of happiness, you see,
is not found in seeking more,
but in developing the capacity to enjoy less.

SOCRATES

I've discovered that the longer you keep a trailer or RV, the fuller it becomes. I used to think that stuff actually reproduced in there. I knew I had only one teakettle...but then there were two. Eventually I had to admit it was my fault, as I am, by nature, something of a pack rat. I've learned I must be on my guard, lest I turn into a hoarder. I *so* don't want to go there.

I must confess that it's way too easy to find that special something that's just perfect for the RV. It's probably the result of stopping at too many cute shops with too much cute stuff while out on the road. And those items add up. Not only that, but over the years I've gotten into the bad practice of putting clothing items I no longer want in my home wardrobe out in the RV. Seriously, why do I think if I don't like a jacket at home, I will like it on the road?

And then there are those tempting camping improvements: You find some upgrade item, like the perfect camp chair, or another piece of cast iron that you know will be absolutely perfect over a campfire. I partially blame the RV industry, because they keep coming up with enticing new stuff. Stuff I really don't need. And extra weight that my RV doesn't need to carry. Overloading is a bad habit, but I know I'm not the only camper who does this.

In fact, it's a reminder that I need to do a couple of things. First, it's time to watch Lucille Ball's neurotic hoarding disorder in *The Long, Long Trailer* again. I have two copies of that video—one for home and one for the road. The scene where Lucy's husband, Desi, hurls jars of preserves and Lucy's rock collection over the cliff is a good visual aid for those of us who overload our RVs.

The second thing I need to do is the yearly spring cleaning. It's not just time to tidy up for camp season; it's also time to clear out the excess. And a weight reduction might help with gas mileage. Now, in case you have similar challenges, I'll share a helpful guideline that not only declutters your camping abode but can also work in your home.

I look over each item, asking myself two questions: (1) Do I use it? (2) Do I love it? If I can't answer yes to at least one question, I toss the item. Here's how: I have two boxes and a trash bag handy. Box one is for giveaways (because someone I know will appreciate the item). Box two is to donate (Habitat for Humanity, Salvation Army, and the like). You know what the trash bag is for.

It's surprising how great it feels to complete this task. I'm sure our RV feels better too—and maybe we'll save some money on gas. Here's another little tip for the road: When I can't resist that adorable moose lamp at the tourist shop, I tell myself that if I bring in something new, I must take out something old. And if I'm not willing to get rid of anything, it's time to start avoiding those cute tourist-trap shops, camping shows, flea markets, and garage sales. No more cleaning out my home closets either. Because really, when it comes to RVs, trailers, and campsites, less is more.

You have succeeded in life when all you really want
is only what you really need.
VERNON HOWARD

TIP FOR THE DAY

Sometimes I don't have time to spring-clean before we head out on our first trip of the season. So when we have an unscheduled free day, I take time to do it at our campsite. I toss the trash and bless the nearest thrift store with a donation.

Entry 49

THE RV PACE

Truth is ever to be found in simplicity,
and not in the multiplicity and confusion of things.

ISAAC NEWTON

As someone who doesn't love housework, I'm always surprised that I don't mind housekeeping when we're out camping. I suppose that's partly because a small space like our RV is fairly easy to clean. In a short time, you get rewarding results. But I think there's something more to it.

I'm sure you've noticed that when you're camping, everything seems to slow down. At least that's how it is for us—once we're settled in. You breathe more deeply. You pause to take in your surroundings—without feeling you're dawdling. I'm convinced that blood pressure levels decrease while we camp—and endorphin levels rise.

I'm not suggesting there's no labor involved in camping. It's just that it doesn't feel like real work to me. Maybe it's because camp chores aren't as demanding as home responsibilities. Or maybe it's just that there aren't the same intrusive distractions, complications, and general anxiety that come with daily living on the home front. Camp life is much more simplified. And for me, simpler is satisfying.

For instance, I love the simplicity of washing the dishes in my RV. Oh, sure, I suppose it's not as easy as putting them into the dishwasher at home. But there's something about the feel of hot soapy water, scrubbing, rinsing, and drying the dishes. I find it soothing. And there's the perk of clean hands when I'm done.

I like doing dishes so much that while we're camping I won't even let my husband help. I usually encourage him to go outside and relax while I'm washing up. I enjoy the alone time. I'll put on music and get in the groove as I wash. Weirdly enough, it's fun.

I've tried to wrap my head around the difference between housework in the RV and back at home. I've asked myself why I can't seem to incorporate my relaxed RV homemaking attitude into our home. I've finally concluded that it's just a matter of pace. I realize that over the years of caring for kids, managing the household, and balancing a career, I've trained myself to complete household tasks very quickly. Probably because my to-do lists always seem to outweigh my available time. And high-speed housecleaning isn't much fun. But, as they say, old habits are hard to break.

Yet I get into the RV and automatically slow way down. Chris and I both do. I'm sure that's just one more reason we love camping. Life is suddenly simpler, and we're no longer driven by the clock. We take our time to complete camp chores. Whether it's chopping wood or washing dishes, we enjoy the process—and we take satisfaction in a completed task. And then we relax.

Even if there are distractions, we tend to welcome them. We take it in stride. It is what it is. And we don't change our slowed-down pace. No hurries, no worries. What needs doing will get done...eventually. It's kind of like *island time*.

I often tell myself that I'm going to practice that same relaxed pace after we get home, but as soon as we're in our house, there are a million things to do and we get pulled right into it. Maybe that's just as well, because it's the lure of the slower, simpler lifestyle that urges us to go camping. And, really, what is wrong with that?

Purity and simplicity are the two wings
with which man soars above the earth
and all temporary nature.
THOMAS À KEMPIS

TIP FOR THE DAY

If you're doing dishes in your RV or trailer and want to keep your gray-water holding tank from filling up too quickly, use a dishpan (or an oversized bowl that doubles as a salad bowl) to catch your rinse water. Then share that water, once it's cooled, with the camp foliage around your campsite.

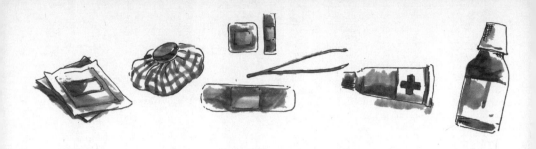

CAMP CATASTROPHES

Traveling is a brutality.
It forces you to trust strangers and to lose sight
of all that familiar comfort of home and friends.
You are constantly off balance.
Nothing is yours except the essential things:
air, sleep, dreams, sea, the sky—
all things tending towards the eternal
or what we imagine of it.

CESARE PAVESE

We should know better than to plan a camping trip in August. But because that's our anniversary month, we've made this mistake—a few times. Eventually we learned that August is not a good month for camping. One of the more obvious reasons is that everyone else and their dogs want to camp in August. Even when you have a reservation—because you made it months ago—you can still get stuck in a crowded, noisy campground.

Not only are there crowds to consider in August, but where we live, it's the height of forest-fire season. And our woodsy cabin home is next to a national forest. But, hey, that's hindsight talking.

Anyway, it's our anniversary—a fairly monumental one too. So we're planning a big trip to Glacier National Park. And, yes, it's August. We have everything ready to go, including a new canoe that we can't wait to try out along the way. Because we need to replace the hitch to our tow car, we delay our trip by one day. Just one day.

While waiting for the hitch, we go out for lunch. On our way we notice something strange in the sky. Two tall smoke chimneys out in the national forest. Because they're highly visible against the cloudless blue sky, we assume that bomber planes will soon be dumping fire repellant on these fires, and they'll easily be extinguished. Think again.

The next morning, we smell smoke as we get ready to leave. We feel confident that these fires surely got nipped in the bud, so we head out. But just in case, we ask a friend with a firefighter son to keep us updated. We've traveled about five hours when we get the phone call. Not only is the fire raging out of control, some evacuations are already in place. Our neighborhood is on high alert.

So we turn around and head for home. The smoke is thick, and the news is bad and getting worse by the hour. We meet with neighbors and everyone exchanges phone information and discusses where we'll go if we're evacuated. But after a couple of days, our evacuation alert level is lowered. We decide that since it is our anniversary tomorrow and our RV is still loaded, why not camp at a nearby lake—and try out that canoe? Since the lake is only two hours away, we can hop right back home if we need to.

We drive to the lake and get settled into a crowded campground. When we try out the canoe, we're disappointed to see the normally pristine lake is infected with some creepy form of fish-killing algae. Not only that, but the smoke from another forest fire is creeping this way. Plus, our cell phones aren't connecting and we're unsure about the forest fire back home.

It's all very unsettling. Then, on our third day, we hear about an unfortunate couple (tent-camped outside of the campgrounds) who've been murdered in the night. And, well, we just want to go home. Although it wasn't a very fun anniversary, it was a memorable one. And we learned that camping in August isn't the best way to celebrate.

Travel far enough, you meet yourself.
DAVID MITCHELL

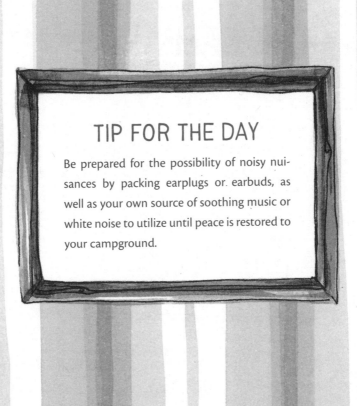

TIP FOR THE DAY

Be prepared for the possibility of noisy nui-
sances by packing earplugs or earbuds, as
well as your own source of soothing music or
white noise to utilize until peace is restored to
your campground.

Entry 51

THE CAMP HOST

A man practices the art of adventure
when he breaks the chain of routine and renews his life
through reading new books, traveling to new places,
making new friends, taking up new hobbies,
and adopting new viewpoints.

WILFRED PETERSON

For us, camping is as much about people as place. And while it's fairly easy to befriend fellow campers, we've learned that camp hosts often enjoy a little befriending too. But sometimes it's not obvious. I think it's simply because these hosts are so used to getting complaints. Most of their interaction with campers happens when something's broken or not working right—or when someone's dog is barking too much.

So it's no wonder that some camp hosts can come across as a bit cool and prickly—at first. But once we get to know them we usually discover they're quite congenial, and often quite interesting too. At least when they have time. Depending on the time of year and number of campers, sometimes they barely have time to say hello. And we try to respect that too. The last thing we want is to make their job more difficult.

During off-season camping on the Oregon coast, we become good friends with two camp hosts—a relationship that continues over several years. Not only do we enjoy spending time with this couple, whenever we call to make a reservation, they do whatever they can to accommodate us. Even on short notice, we usually get to stay in our favorite seaside campsite. We even exchange Christmas cards.

It's always fun to catch up with our coastal camp host friends. And they're a great resource. They might share about a new restaurant down the road, or where there's good clamming, or where the perch are running. They might give us the weekly weather forecast or introduce us to some campers they think we'd like to get acquainted with.

Being friends with the camp hosts makes it feel like we're family, like we have a home away from home. That makes our camping experience even more fun. Even after our favorite campground is sold, we remain in touch with our host friends.

When we visit new campgrounds—especially when we plan to be there for a spell—we get to know the camp hosts. We like to discover where they're from and how they got into camp hosting. It's almost always an interesting story.

And who knows? Maybe we'll try being camp hosts someday. We've talked about how that might be a fun retirement job. If we do become hosts, I hope our campers will be friendly to us. Because friends and campgrounds go together like s'mores and a campfire. Why would you want to camp without them?

> Since there is nothing so well worth having as friends,
> never lose a chance to make them.
>
> FRANCESCO GUICCIARDINI

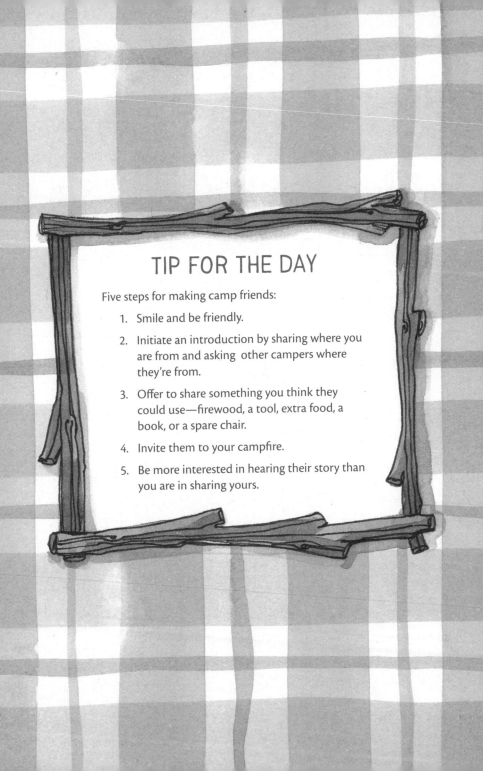

TIP FOR THE DAY

Five steps for making camp friends:

1. Smile and be friendly.

2. Initiate an introduction by sharing where you are from and asking other campers where they're from.

3. Offer to share something you think they could use—firewood, a tool, extra food, a book, or a spare chair.

4. Invite them to your campfire.

5. Be more interested in hearing their story than you are in sharing yours.

VINTAGE FUN

Creativity is just connecting things.
When you ask creative people how they did something,
they feel a little guilty because they didn't really do it.
They just saw something.
It seemed obvious to them after a while.
That's because they were able to connect experiences
they'd had and synthesize new things.

STEVE JOBS

One of my secret desires has been to restore an old vintage trailer. I'm not sure how or why this crazy idea originated, but when I spot a 1960s Oasis trailer parked by the highway with a for-sale sign, I'm all in. And the price is right. I call the owner, who tells me it's unlocked and to go ahead and look inside. When I see the interior, including bright orange appliances, I can just imagine it.

To my pleased surprise, Chris thinks it's a good idea too. Before I know it we're hauling home what most people would think was a great big hunk of junk. But I see the potential. And I tell Chris, a handyman who can fix almost anything, "This is my project. I want to do it myself." Because he has his own projects, he doesn't argue.

For the next couple of weeks, I'm obsessed with cleaning and sanding and painting and fixing and replacing things. I remove all the hardware and paint the solid-wood kitchen cabinets a cheerful turquoise, which looks fabulous with the orange appliances. I'm giving the interior sort of a Southwest theme, which I think will be charming.

I sew cute curtains and reupholster the banquette and the sofa bed. I make pillows and gather a fun collection of orange and turquoise accessories, fully outfitting this charming vintage trailer. I even find some vintage paint-by-number pictures that look just perfect. I get a turquoise teapot and enamelware dishes that look vintage. I put all the pieces together, and it feels like a playhouse—and so adorable!

Although my plan is to sell my vintage trailer, I'm not sure I can part with this cutie-pie. Of course I know it's too small for us to use. Remember, I have an extra-tall husband. Plus we already have the motor home. But since it's late in the selling season and I still haven't finished the exterior, I decide to hold on to it through the winter.

When weather permits, I work on the exterior, and eventually the trailer is pretty much finished.

Now I have no excuse to keep it much longer. Well, except that it's been my "baby" and I really do love it. But I know it's taking up space and it's time to let it go. I place an ad on Craigslist, and it's not long before I get some calls.

I must say my sweet trailer couldn't have found a sweeter family. The mother, an artist, totally appreciates the ambiance and aesthetics—and the dad and boys like it too. It's hard to explain why that's so important to me, but I want my trailer to go to a good home—and I'm sure this one is.

Now, when I'm out driving through the countryside, I'm keeping a lookout for another fixer-upper vintage trailer. In the meantime, I occupy myself by writing a novel about my fun restoration experience. It's called *The Happy Camper*.

One of the things that attracts me to vintage
and antique things is they have stories,
and even if I don't know the stories, I make them up.
MARY KAY ANDREWS

TIP FOR THE DAY

Most vintage trailers don't have a bathroom. An easy, inexpensive porta potty can be created from a five-gallon bucket and a toilet seat. And you might consider setting up an affordable solar-shower with a shower curtain outside your trailer. For more fun camping tips, check out *Glamping with MaryJane* (my favorite vintage camping book).

Entry 53

BREAKING CAMP

A journey is a gesture inscribed in space,
it vanishes even as it's made.
You go from one place to another place,
and on to somewhere else again,
and already behind you there is no trace
that you were ever there.

DAMON GALGUT

My husband and I made a rule for ourselves more than 40 years ago. *Leave it better than we found it.* To start with, we applied this principle to our first rental homes. We always did some kind of improvements, whether we lived in an apartment, duplex, or house. Sometimes we painted or repaired something; sometimes we planted flowers. But no matter what, we always left the place cleaner than when we came. It was satisfying to us. This carried over, in a big way, to homes we later purchased. Even before HGTV we were doing major renovations in our homes. And, of course, we've applied this rule to trailers and RVs too. Every single one has received some kind of improvement.

Not surprisingly, we bring this attitude camping with us. We always try to leave our campsite slightly nicer than we find it. That could mean picking up someone else's trash, cleaning a grungy fire pit, pruning dead foliage, leaving some leftover firewood, or even pulling a few weeds. And if a campsite is impeccable when we arrive—and that sometimes happens—we simply make sure it's just as impeccable when we depart.

I usually have mixed feelings when it's time to break camp. On one hand, if we've been there awhile, I'm ready to move on. I might even be ready to go home. But, if we've had a really great time, I'm also a bit sad. This reminds me to get a camp brochure or website information, and to write down the numbers of preferred campsites—in the hopes we'll return someday.

On departure day, we always try to give ourselves plenty of time to pack up, clean up, and say a few goodbyes. Then our goal is to evacuate our space an hour or so before departure time. Camp hosts seem to appreciate that. Probably because it helps with the "rush hour" that can occur when numerous campers try to exit simultaneously. Especially if they all need to empty their holding tanks—and that's a line we like to avoid whenever possible.

I like to think our *leave it better than we found it* rule applies to all areas of our lives—not just campsites and homes. I hope the friends we make while camping feel better for having met us. I know that's how I feel when we make new camp friends. It's as if my life's been enriched. Whether we share on a deep spiritual level or simply enjoy a few laughs and stories around the campfire, I hope our time together is positive for everyone. And because I'm a writer (and we always bring books), Chris is quick to share my books before we go.

Our parting prayer, always, is that we have left this place better than we found it.

I wandered everywhere,
through cities and countries wide.
And everywhere I went,
the world was on my side.

ROMAN PAYNE

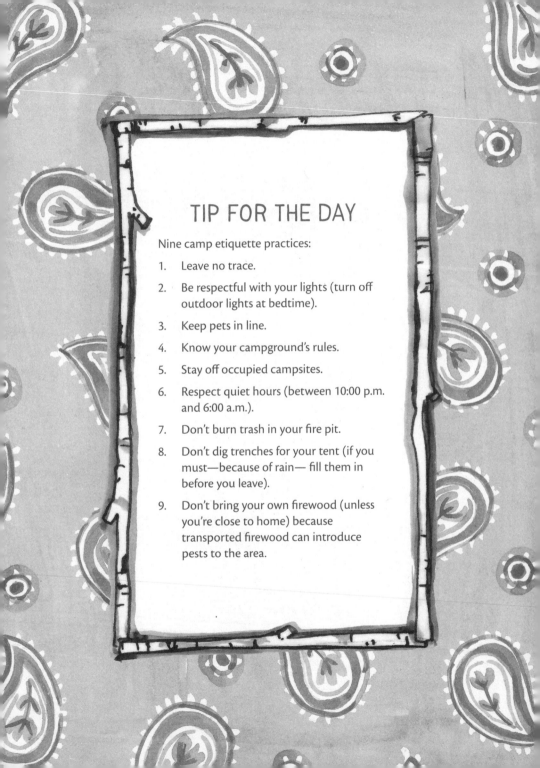

TIP FOR THE DAY

Nine camp etiquette practices:

1. Leave no trace.

2. Be respectful with your lights (turn off outdoor lights at bedtime).

3. Keep pets in line.

4. Know your campground's rules.

5. Stay off occupied campsites.

6. Respect quiet hours (between 10:00 p.m. and 6:00 a.m.).

7. Don't burn trash in your fire pit.

8. Don't dig trenches for your tent (if you must—because of rain— fill them in before you leave).

9. Don't bring your own firewood (unless you're close to home) because transported firewood can introduce pests to the area.

Entry 54
THE NEXT TRIP

Here I am, safely returned over those peaks
from a journey far more beautiful and strange
than anything I had hoped for or imagined—
how is it that this safe return brings such regret?

PETER MATHIESSON

Part of the fun of camping is dreaming about where your next trip will take you. Especially if it's midwinter and both you and your RV are buried beneath several feet of snow. That's when I want to start planning a cross-country trip to the Florida Keys. Maybe someday we will do it.

I've discovered that as we get older, our dreams seem to get bigger. Our bucket list used to be pretty long—we wanted to visit the major national parks, and we've done a few. But now we've added a Southern trip and an East Coast fall foliage trip and a Canada to Alaska trip. And I'm sure we're not done.

Chris and I both love maps and atlases. We like imagining what roads we'll take next time and determining the best time to visit certain regions. But I must admit that we are not, by nature, the best planners. Sometimes it's been more fun to be serendipitous. If you're camping in the off-season, that might work, but I'm discovering that preparing a trip plan and making reservations can be more peaceful in the long run. Especially since there seems to be more and more campers out there each year.

Chris and I have also gone back and forth over which is the best way to travel and to camp. Of course, we've given up tent camping for good. Well, unless it's our oversized wall tent—and if it had all the comforts of home. That might be fun. But as far as taking extended trips, we still discuss the differences between trailer versus motor home. I must admit that the jury is still out on this one. Gas mileage is about the same, and the length they take on the road and campsite is similar.

For now, I lean toward keeping our old Bounder motor home. I think we should run it as long as it wants to go. Just like us. I just want to be sure we keep going out there. We've recently discussed a trip that would take us through western Canada and on up to Alaska. Our research begins by talking to others who have already made this long trek. We're gathering information and starting to put together a plan. But we probably won't be able to implement it for a year or two.

Meanwhile, we want to continue exploring closer places with shorter trips...and to gather more stories, and more friends. And God willing and the creek don't rise, we'll take those bigger trips in the next couple of years. I'm pretty sure it will take the rest of our lives to see everything that's on our ever-growing bucket list—if that's even possible—but I do look forward to it.

I absolutely love it when I see a pair of elderly campers out there enjoying themselves and the world and people around them. I sincerely hope that is us someday!

The woods are lovely, dark and deep,
But I have promises to keep,
And miles to go before I sleep,
And miles to go before I sleep.

ROBERT FROST

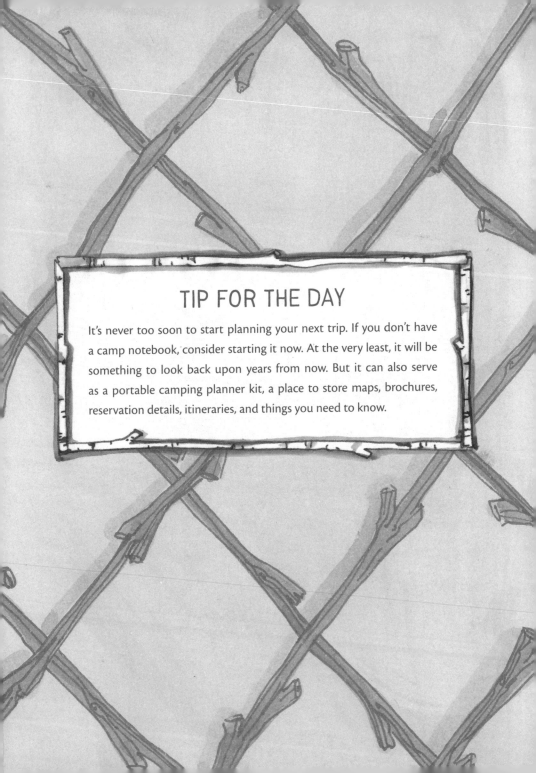

TIP FOR THE DAY

It's never too soon to start planning your next trip. If you don't have a camp notebook, consider starting it now. At the very least, it will be something to look back upon years from now. But it can also serve as a portable camping planner kit, a place to store maps, brochures, reservation details, itineraries, and things you need to know.

A Final Word to My Fellow Campers

Thank you for taking this journey with me. I hope you've been encouraged or inspired or even simply entertained with my little camping stories. I also hope we'll cross paths out there in the big camping world. It could happen! If you spot Chris and me somewhere in our old Bounder, please stop and say hello. Who knows, I might even give you a book—or share s'mores!

In the meantime, I wish you happy trails, a warm campfire, new friends, inspiring experiences...and a newfound appreciation for the beautiful world our loving Creator has given to all of us.

About the Author

Melody Carlson has written 200 books for teens, women, and children, with more than five million copies sold. She's won several awards from the Romance Writers of America, the Evangelical Christian Publishers Association, *Christian Retailing* magazine, and other national organizations. Melody and her husband have two grown sons and make their home in the Pacific Northwest. You can connect with Melody at www.melodycarlson.com.

Some Melody Carlson books you might enjoy while on the road...

The Happy Camper	Homeward on the Oregon Trail series
Courting Mr. Emerson	The Mulligan Sisters series
	Legacy of Sunset Cove series

Cover design and hand lettering by Kristi Smith–Juicebox Designs

Interior design by Kristi Smith

Gathered Around the Campfire
Text copyright © 2020 by Melody A. Carlson; artwork copyright © by Michal Sparks
Published by Harvest House Publishers
Eugene, Oregon 97408
www.harvesthousepublishers.com

ISBN 978-0-7369-7975-7 (pbk)
ISBN 978-0-7369-7976-4 (eBook)

Library of Congress Cataloging-in-Publication Data
Names: Carlson, Melody, author.
Title: Gathered around the campfire / Melody A Carlson.
Description: Eugene, Oregon : Harvest House Publishers, [2020]
Identifiers: LCCN 2019034733 (print) | LCCN 2019034734 (ebook) | ISBN
    9780736979757 (paperback) | ISBN 9780736979764 (ebook)
Subjects: LCSH: Camping. | Outdoor recreation. | Family recreation.
Classification: LCC GV191.7 .C375 2020 (print) | LCC GV191.7 (ebook) |
    DDC 796.54--dc23
LC record available at https://lccn.loc.gov/2019034733
LC ebook record available at https://lccn.loc.gov/2019034734

Printed in the United States of America

20 21 22 23 24 25 26 27 28 / VP/ 10 9 8 7 6 5 4 3 2 1